To our beloved children and grandchildren
who carry our legacy of faith, strength and honor
with them for generations to come.

...and the truth will set you free.
—John 8:32

Ay Nicaragua, Nicaragüita,
La flor mas linda de mi querer,
Abonada con la bendita,
Nicaragüita, sangre de Diriangén.
Ay Nicaragua sos mas dulcita,
Que la mielita de Tamagas,
Pero ahora que ya sos libre,
Nicaragüita, yo te quiero mucho mas.
Pero ahora que ya sos libre,
Nicaragüita, yo te quiero mucho mas.
—Famous Folk Song "Nicaragua, Nicaragüita"
written by Carlos Mejía Godoy

TABLE of CONTENTS

PART I
Nicaragua

Chapter 1: "Heaven Touched Earth"   2

Chapter 2: Worldwide Influence   5

Chapter 3: Public Schools in Nicaragua   7

Chapter 4: Max Factor Makeup and Catalina Swimsuits   9

Chapter 5: Meeting My "Maverick"   17

Chapter 6: SS Michelangelo   19

Chapter 7: Prank Chester   20

Chapter 8: Sweet Serenade   21

Chapter 9: 6.25 Earthquake   22

Chapter 10: Somocistas and Sandinistas   24

Chapter 11: *El Trompo*   30

Chapter 12: Cadet Training   34

Chapter 13: Sitting on a Powder Keg   43

Chapter 14: "The Apocalypse"   45

Chapter 15: "Makeshift Prison"   46

Chapter 16: "Chestercito"   47

Chapter 17: Playas de Pochomil   51

Chapter 18: Surviving the Angel of Death   52

Chapter 19: "You May Kiss the Bride!"   53

Chapter 20: "Born-Again" Christian   55

Chapter 21: Chester Lassos Stork Again   56

Chapter 22: Bona-Fide Civil War   61

Chapter 23: "We Can't Win!"   64

Chapter 24: La Nica Airlines   65

PART II
Louisiana

Chapter 1: New Orleans International Airport   68

Chapter 2: "An Act of Barbarism"   70

Chapter 3: "Out of Harm's Way"   71

Chapter 4: *Nacatamales*   76

Chapter 5: Asylum   78

Chapter 6: The Pitfalls of the Word-Faith Movement   80

Chapter 7: Hoops and Hurdles to Get My Commercial Pilot's License   82

Chapter 8: Kissing Rocks, Bushes and Debris   83

Chapter 9: Crop-Dusting in Arkansas   85

Chapter 10: A Hare Krishna Temple and a Flight to Venezuela   87

Chapter 11: "Old Faithful"   93

Chapter 12: Mardi Gras at the Marriott (Rated-R)   95

Chapter 13: Sugar Cane Fields   97

Chapter 14: Sizzling Cajun Barbeque Chicken   100

Chapter 15: Gushing Blood and an Attempted Carjacking   103

Chapter 16: Cowboy   105

PART III
California

Chapter 1: The Lord Smiled Down on Us   109

Chapter 2: Establish a Clientele   111

Chapter 3: Back to Studying   112

Chapter 4: Thrive Not Just Survive   113

Chapter 5: Renewing Our Wedding Vows   114

Chapter 6: Highly Recommended   116

Chapter 7: Pulkrabek   117

Chapter 8: "It Was the Best of Times, It Was the Worst of Times"   119

Chapter 9: Set Up, Beaten and Mugged   120

Chapter 10: "It's a Girl!"   124

Chapter 11: Naturalized Citizens   130

Chapter 12: A Paranoid Escape Artist   133

Chapter 13: Glorious Homes Full   136

Chapter 14: Overcoming Stereotypes   138

Chapter 15: ¡Viva Las Vegas!   139

Chapter 16: Glorious Homes #2   140

Chapter 17: Friends and Family   143

Chapter 18: A New Decade   144

Chapter 19: Busy Bees   148

Chapter 20: Honoring Cpl. Rolando A. Delagneau Vivas   153

Chapter 21: Platinum Blond   154

Chapter 22: Growing Pains   156

Chapter 23: Church Bells Chime   164

Chapter 24: Salvation   167

Chapter 25: Endless Summer   169
Chapter 26: "Party Like It's 1999!"   174
Chapter 27: A New Hope, A New Decade, A New Century   180
Chapter 28: Radical Islamic Jihadists   185
Chapter 29: Never Lose Faith   187
Chapter 30: Nicaraguan and Norwegian Worlds Collide   188
Chapter 31: Hurricane Katrina: Bursting New Orleans's Levees   192
Chapter 32: Zela Ursulina "Lina"   194
Chapter 33: "First Comes Love, Then Comes Marriage…"   199
Chapter 34: A Military Funeral   204
Chapter 35: Miss Nicaragua   206
Chapter 36: "Gift from God"   210
Chapter 37: Prostate Cancer   220
Chapter 38: National Certified Medical Assistant (NCMA)   221
Chapter 39: Chester Delagneau, B.A., M.A., M.A.   222
Chapter 40: Mariann and Martha   225
Chapter 41: "…And Then Comes a Baby in a Baby Carriage"   227
Chapter 42: Remembering Martin Hinzie and Luis Sevilla   233
Chapter 43: Josefana "Fanny" Norma   235
Chapter 44: Linkin Joie Delagneau   236
Chapter 45: Same Diagnosis, Different Conclusion   238
Chapter 46: Sold!   240
Chapter 47: *Chi Mangia Bene, Vive Bene*   242
Chapter 48: Book Launch Party!   243
Chapter 49: Angelito Gabriel   245
Chapter 50: Miracle Baby   250
Chapter 51: "32 Years of Loyal Dedicated Service"   256
Chapter 52: 4th of July   258

PART IV
Appendices

Appendix A: Editor's Cut Pictures   261
Appendix B: Glorious Homes' Letters of Recommendation   282
Appendix C: Crystal, Jean Pierre and Chester Jr.'s Letters of
            Gratitude   289
Appendix D: "Suitcase of One" Poem   292
Appendix E: "The Gardener" Poetic Prose   294

PART I
Nicaragua

Chapter 1: "Heaven Touched Earth"

AMONG THE TOBACCO FARMS AND COFFEE PLANTATIONS OF NICARAGUA, I was born. On March 13, 1951, the little town of Diriamba, Nicaragua, just south of the capital Managua, increased its population by one. My birth certificate reads "Myriam Mendieta Mendieta,"

My mother about 45-years-old. Managua.

on account of my mother marrying her cousin, Pedro Pablo Mendieta Gutierrez (born early 1930s; died August 1981). My mother, Berta Julia Mendieta Flores,[1] also born in Diriamba (May 15, 1926; died October 17, 1994), moved to Managua when I was only three years old. She was a strong, independent woman to leave her alcoholic and abusive husband behind, especially with a flock of chicks by her side. I was the second youngest of five sisters: Martha, Zela Ursulina ("Lina"), Josefana ("Fanny") Norma, me and Sylvia.

---

[1] What I remember most about her is that she was extremely caring, especially to those in need. In this way, she was just like her mother and father. Her mother, Prudencia Flores, used to cook for and bring food to prisoners at the local jail. And her father, Joseph Stephen Mendieta Vela, was well-known for his compassion to those in need.

My biological father with his brothers. Left to right: Tio Orlando, Tio "Mincho," Tio "Toño," Tio Juan, and my father, Pedro Pablo Mendieta Gutierrez. Diriamba. Circa 1970.

As a little girl I loved to play with dolls and sew clothes for them. I learned the art of sewing from my mother, who was a professional seamstress. I remember my mother being a great provider for us girls. She would get up early every morning with the aid of our neighbor's raucous rooster and make us all breakfast: corn tortillas, *cuajada fresca* (soft milk curd), and *gallo pinto* (fried rice and beans mixed together).

A typical day for me in Managua consisted of going to school from 8 a.m.–12 p.m., coming home for two hours to eat and nap, and then returning to school from 2 p.m.–4 p.m. I would do my homework as soon as I got home and then it was time for dinner before bedtime. Fanny was my roommate and my playmate before "lights out." Our favorite games were Jacks and Patty Cake.

My favorite subject was grammar and my favorite sport was volleyball. In general, I was an obedient child to my mother and a good student at school.[2] I loved the evenings when Martha would recite poetry at the dinner table while I perched on the stairs and rested my head against the coolness of the wall. Her recitations instilled in me an appreciation for the beautiful words of poets like Rubén Dario, Sor Juana Inés de la Cruz, Gabriela Mistral and Pablo Neruda.

I was an extremely sensitive and spiritual young girl. Whenever I would see someone with whom no one else wanted to play, I made it my mission to befriend that person and make her feel included.

---

[2] My sisters would often tell me that I was precocious. And it turned out to be true. When I took my matriculation exam for second grade, I scored off the charts. So I bypassed second grade and went directly into third grade.

Also, I enjoyed going to mass on Sundays and I would pray whenever I felt the situation called for God's merciful intervention.

Me (7) with my friend Irvin Ernesto Bunge Garcia (7). Managua. 1958.

Nature always had a way of making an impression on my sensibilities, particularly the ocean. I remember going to the beach when I was five years old before school started in January.[3] My mother drove us girls to visit her mother in Diriamba. From there we took an oxen-pulled cart to see the Pacific Ocean for the first time.

"Heaven touched earth" is what I thought when my eyes poured over the calm watery horizon. I saw foam everywhere. It was as if the clouds had fallen from the sky. As far as the eyes could see, one infinite point to my left and another to my right, and a couple hundred feet outward, a white spume like a cotton blanket covered the salty sea. I loved everything about the ocean, playing in the water and on the shore, the feeling of the soft sand on my feet and the smell of the fresh marine air.

Sadly, it was the death of my favorite cousin, Lucia Figueroa Mendieta, that negatively affected my infatuation with the ocean. When she was about 21-years-old, she was caught in a strong rip current and drowned. After that day, I've kept a respectable distance from her seductive yet dangerous power.

---

[3] The schools in Nicaragua then started on the first day of the calendar year.

Chapter 2: Worldwide Influence

IT'S IMPORTANT NOT TO UNDERESTIMATE THE EFFECTS THE MENDIETAS have had on Latin America. In the 1500s, there were four brothers that came from Vitoria Mendietan, Spain, to evangelize the gospel of Jesus Christ in Diriamba (Nicaragua), Mexico and Cuba. One of the descendants of these brothers became the president of Cuba.

The Latin culture is an artistic culture and Diriamba is a shining example of its creativity, best known for being *la cuna* or "the birthplace" of El Güegüense—Nicaraguan folklore combining music, dance and theatre. Amilcar Antonio Mendieta Baltodano, the son of the youngest of five brothers, was heavily influenced by the colorful Güegüense culture. His paintings are in display in many parts of the world, such as United States, Sweden, Germany, France, Japan and Columbia.

My cousin, Amilcar Mendieta, exhibiting his painting of the immortalized Macho Ratón, one of the characters of the first play of Nicaraguan literature "El Güegüense," at the inauguration of the "Nicaragua-Diriambina Culture" exhibition in Germany. July 11, 2015.

Salvador Mendieta Cascante (1882–1958), another influential Mendieta, is the brother of my great grandfather, Alejo Mendieta Cascante. Salvador is known for quite a few things, most notably his political and literary accomplishments. During the administration of José Madriz Rodríguez from 1909–1910, he was secretary to the president and was sent to Costa Rica to promote the unionization of Central America. Then, during the administration of Juan Bautista Sacasa from 1933–1934, he served as Inspector General of Public Instruction. At this time, he was also Professor of History of Central America at the Ramírez Goyena Institute, as well as Professor of Constitutional and Administrative Law at the Managua Law School. Salvador was also a prolific writer, penning more than 1,500 pages in his monumental study of what he calls *La Enfermedad de Centro-America* (*The Illness of Central America*), in which he diagnosis the disease or weakness of character of Central America as a collective *abulia* (lack of initiative), as well as poverty and moral cowardice, among other things.

My great great uncle, Dr. Salvador
Mendieta Cascante (1882-1958). Photo
taken from "La República Centroamérica
en la vision de Salvador Mendieta y el
Partido Unionista Centroamericano,"
elpulso.hn/?p=8497.

The flag of Nicaragua was first adopted in 1908 but not made official until 1971. In the coat of arms, the five volcanoes represent the
union of the five Central American countries (excluding Panama and Belize). In 1838, the first to become independent countries were
Nicaragua, Honduras, Costa Rica and Guatemala, followed by El Salvador in 1841. Traditionally, the two blue stripes represent the
Pacific Ocean and the Caribbean Sea, but a more modern interpretation favors them as justice and loyalty. The white stripe indicates
peace. The triangle symbolizes equality. And the rainbow signifies liberty.

Chapter 3: Public Schools in Nicaragua

PUBLIC SCHOOLS IN NICARAGUA were steeped in the default religion of the country: Catholicism. The only difference with public and parochial schools is that public schools were free, barring paying for one's own books and school supplies.

Once I graduated from my elementary school—Colegio Bautista de Managua—I went on to high school. (In Nicaragua at the time, there was no middle school. So once a student graduates from elementary school—grades First through Sixth—she attends the next echelon of education, which is high school—grades Seventh through Twelfth.)

Unfortunately, I was unable to graduate high school because of my stepfather's premature death. He paid for me to attend parochial school, so when he died, my dreams of graduating high school died with him. But an unusual set of circumstances transpired that set me on a new course of education, albeit, not academic.

Me (14) in my favorite dress with my sister, Fanny, at *Las Piedrecitas*. Managua. 1965.

Me (almost 15) receiving my diploma from Director Wilson for graduating sixth grade at Colegio Bautista. Managua.
February 28, 1966.

Six days before my 15th birthday. Managua. 1966.

Chapter 4: Max Factor Makeup and Catalina Swimsuits

"MYRIAM, TURN THIS WAY!" "Tilt your head to the side." "Rest your hand on your hip." Flash!-Flash!-Flash! Quick change into next outfit. Mascara coating long lashes. Scarlet lipstick changing to subtle beige. Such were the commands and routines of my modeling days in the late 1960s. Flipping through glossy fashion magazines as a child, I never fancied that one day I, too, would grace advertisements for such reputable brands as Max Factor, Helena Rubinstein and Catalina Swimsuits. But when a neighbor suggested I explore a career in modeling, the timing could not have been more perfect.

I went to *Foto Luminton* to get my picture taken for my sixteenth birthday. Managua. 1967.

9

El pasado martes 23 de los corrientes fue ofrecido un elegante cóctel en el Club Internacional en honor de la Srita. MARTHA GARZA. Consejera Internacional de Belleza de Max Factor con motivo de su reciente ingreso al país. Aparecen en la gráfica de Aragón en el orden acostumbrado: Srita. Martha Marenco, Srita. Miriam Mendieta, Sra. Paquita de Bardají, Sra. Sofía Montiel, Srita. Martha Garza, Srita. Sonia Benavente C. y Srita. Lesbia Alvarado G.

Me (16), second from the left, representing Max Factor as a beauty consultant at a cocktail party at *Club Internacional* in the Grand Hotel. Managua. 1967.

Me (17) modeling Helena Rubinstein makeup. Managua. 1968.

With five daughters to provide for, my mother faced a constant financial burden. Hoping that modeling could provide a way to ease that burden, I eagerly explored this new possibility. My strong work ethic helped me establish a name and reputation in the modeling industry that opened up many opportunities. I took pride that I was able to do what I set out to accomplish: provide my mother with financial assistance.

My mother, believing in my modeling career, suggested that more opportunities could be found in the cosmopolitan wonderland of New York City. With my older sister, Martha, already living there, it provided the perfect opportunity for Fanny and me to make the trip. I thought living in our capital city of Managua would prepare me for what lay ahead, but New York City overwhelmed me with its grandiosity and pulsating, relentless energy. I was so glad to have my sisters by my side.

Me (18) modeling Catalina bathing suit. Playas de Pochomil. 1969.

Me (19) modeling for world-renowned photographer Hernán Barquero, Jr. Playas de Pochomil. 1970.

As I waited to hear about modeling jobs, I attended a local high school in Manhattan and took classes in mathematics, United States history, science and typewriting. Determined to expand my knowledge of the English language, I took my Spanish-English dictionary with me wherever I went: strolling through Greenwich Village, visiting the Metropolitan Museum of Art, relaxing on a grassy knoll in Central Park or riding the subway. Anytime I'd see an English word I didn't know, I'd whip out my dictionary, look up the word and commit it to memory. The years between 1970–1971 were filled with wonder but my homesickness grew too strong, so I returned home in November '71.

Me (19) at typewriting class. New York. 1970.

Me (19) in a photo booth after recently arriving to Manhattan. New York. 1970.

Me (19) with Ursula Andress, Swiss actress most famous for her role as Bond Girl Honey Ryder. New York. 1970.

Me (19) modeling for a New York magazine.
New York. 1970.

Me (19) in Central Park. New York. December 1970.

Me (19) modeling in Central Park. New York. 1971.

When I arrived back home, I started working for a very well known hotel at the time, called Hotel Balmoral, to assist in public relations at the Mercedes International Airport (now known as Augusto Cesar Sandino International Airport), while continuing to model on the side.

Me (20) when I returned home to Managua from New York. 1971.

Chapter 5: Meeting My "Maverick"

ON JANUARY 29, 1972, I met Chester José Delagneau Gonzalez, both a military pilot for the Nicaraguan Air Force and a Nicaraguan crop-dusting pilot, who would become my future husband. This year proved to be unforgettable for many reasons besides meeting Chester.

At the Munich Olympics, 11 Israeli athletes were murdered by Arab terrorists; five White House operatives were arrested for wiretapping the offices of the Democratic National Committee's headquarters (a.k.a., Watergate Scandal); and in Northern Ireland, 14 unarmed Catholic protestors were gunned down by the British army (a.k.a., Bloody Sunday). More inspiringly, American swimmer, Mark Spitz, won a record seven gold medals at the Munich Olympics; biological warfare was banned by world leaders; and American Bobby Fischer beat Russian Boris Spassky to become the World Chess Champion.

In January, Marta Cole, Chester's friend, arranged for his cousin and me to go with them on a double date to the grand opening of a new restaurant/nightclub—El Ron Ron.

After that time, Chester and I would occasionally meet to talk as friends. (It had been only three months since the passing of his fiancé, Marta Manfut, so he was not quite yet ready to get intimately involved with anyone. But we continued to spend time together.) Slowly, over the course of several months, our friendship blossomed into a romantic relationship.

It was just before *Semana Santa* ("Holy Week") that we confessed our love to one another. For the next five months we spent every moment we could together. Chester worked seven days a week crop-dusting and I worked for the Hotel Balmoral, Monday through Friday. That meant that the nights were ours.

We spent the limited time we had going to movies and eating at restaurants. One of our favorite places to eat dinner was Los Ranchos—famous for their *churrascos* (grilled skirt steak) and *chimichurri*.

Occasionally, on the weekends, we enjoyed frequenting our favorite beaches, Playas de Pochomil and Montelimar. That spring and summer was the best time of my life! Imagine my conflicting emotions when I was asked to model in Italy at the end of the summer, knowing it meant leaving Chester for a time. I felt like a real-life Sandra Dee at the beginning of the movie Grease, when she sings, "Summer loving had me a blast. Summer loving happened so fast…."

Me (21) in the spumy waters of Playas de Pochomil. It was during this time that Chester and I swore our love to each other. Spring 1972.

Chapter 6: SS Michelangelo

I LEFT NICARAGUA TO GO TO NEW YORK IN AUGUST OF '72. From New York I took a transatlantic cruise ship called the SS Michelangelo to Rome, Italy. I was a 21-year-old country girl headed to new horizons. I remember the ship being enormous and elegant. On board, I met a

friendly and affluent American couple. The woman took me under her wing asking me to join them for meals and activities during the extent of our trip. I felt like God had put an angel on board just for me. Two weeks later, we arrived at the port of Italy.

Feeling exhausted by the time I checked in to my hotel, I went straight to bed. Strangely, when I awoke the next morning, instead of feeling excited to be there, I felt terribly homesick. I began to wonder what I was doing thousands of miles away from my amor, Chester. So I did the unthinkable: I left, immediately, to see him.

Cocktail Hour on the SS Michelangelo. The captain offered my American friend and I drinks. August 1972.

Chapter 7: Prank Chester

I MISSED CHESTER SO MUCH that when I arrived back to Nicaragua, I flagged down a taxi driver to take me straight to Chester's house. When I got there, he wasn't home; he was crop-dusting. But I got to see his family who were all excited to see me. They told me to wait there for him, so I did.

Just before he walked in, we decided to play a prank on him. They wanted me to sit with my back toward the entrance, so he wouldn't recognize me. As he entered and saw a strange woman with long, beautiful black hair sitting in his house, he wondered what was happening. Everyone started laughing, including me. The gig was up. Chester received me in his arms with a tight embrace. We both cried.

That night we celebrated by going to our favorite restaurant, Los Ranchos. From that point forward we started a serious relationship vowing not to see other people and never to separate from one another again. Little did we know what the future would hold.

Chapter 8: Sweet Serenade

OUR COURTING RELATIONSHIP CONSISTED OF CHESTER WOOING ME by having professional singers serenade me. Several times, he hired them to sing outside my mother's house around 2 a.m. This, of course, woke everyone up, but we all loved it.

One of the things I delighted in most at this time, which consequently made my mother furious, was when Chester performed acrobatic maneuvers with his plane, such as barrel rolls, over our house, once he was done crop-dusting. It literally made our house shake!

Speaking of shaking, a few months later, we encountered the worst earthquake in Nicaragua's history. Saturday, December 23, 1972, would be a day that would live in infamy for all Nicaragüenses: that date is the anniversary of the Nicaraguan earthquake that leveled downtown Managua, the country's capital.

Chapter 9: 6.25 Earthquake

Aftermath of 1972 Managua earthquake. Aerial photograph of Managua shows smoldering rubble. Taken from 3,000 feet by National Aeronautics and Space Administration (NASA) C-130. Photo courtesy of United States Geological Survey (USGS) used by National Oceanic and Atmospheric Association (NOAA) scientists to evaluate damage patterns.

EARLIER THAT SAME DAY Chester buried his grandmother, Carolina Gonzalez Suarez. He wanted to meet up later that night. However, since I had an early curfew I wasn't able to join him.

To relieve stress, Chester went dancing at the Plaza Nightclub. At exactly 12:29 a.m., he felt the earthquake on the dance floor, while I experienced it at home. My brother-in-law, José Felix Garcia, a volunteer firefighter at the time, told me that Managua was destroyed. Immediately, I became deeply concerned because the epicenter of the quake was near the Plaza Nightclub.

Managua's 6.25 magnitude earthquake killed more than 10,000 people and left 250,000 homeless. I remember that no one celebrated Christmas that year. It was sheer chaos. The only visible light at night came from fires (gas explosions?) that burned out of control. To make matters worse, the water supply was cut off so there was no water to drink or to help fight fires. And the electricity was systematically knocked out. The only way to communicate with the outside world was with ham radios.[4]

---

[4] United Press International, "Thousands Dead as Quakes Strike Nicaraguan City," *New York Times*, Sunday, December 24, 1972, front page.

The following day General Anastasio Somoza Debayle, the head of the National Guard and the President of Nicaragua, ordered an evacuation of Managua that was largely ignored. Sadly, the government failed to supply dietary reliefs and there was little to no medical care for those in need.

At this point, please allow me to give a brief history lesson about the earthquake and its socio-political effects. Costa Rica was the first Central American country to send aid. United States' President, Richard Nixon, sent Somoza aid to help rebuild Managua. Relief came in the form of food, medicine, tents and purification equipment that totaled $3,000,000. According to the *New York Times*, "Political moderates and even friends of the Government were angered by the way the Somozas saw the disaster and reconstruction [of Managua] as a business opportunity."[5] This misuse of relief for selfish reasons "grew to such proportions that several foreign governments complained repeatedly...."[6] Even some in the Roman Catholic Church began to speak out against the government.[7]

---

[5] Alan Riding, "Respectable Rebels Threaten Somoza Dynasty," *New York Times*, Sunday, January 29, 1978, pg. 147.
[6] Ibid.
[7] Tim Merrill, "Nicaragua: A Country Study," ed. James D. Rudolph (Washington, D.C.: Library of Congress, Federal Research Division, 1994), xxxi, https://www.loc.gov/item/94021664/ (accessed July 18, 2020).

Chapter 10: Somocistas and Sandinistas

Meeting before State Dinner at the White House in Washington, D.C., on June 2, 1971. Left to right: U.S. President—Richard M. Nixon; Nicaraguan President—Anastasio Somoza Debayle; and White House Chief of Staff—Alexander M. Haig, Jr. Photo courtesy of U.S. National Archives and Records Administration. Photo taken by Jack E. Kightlinger (1932–2009), White House News Photographer who worked under five administrations. Photo adapted.

TWO IMPORTANT EVENYS OCCURRED IN THE '70s. First, human rights activists, both in Nicaragua and the United States, condemned Somoza and fomented insurrection against Somoza's regime throughout Nicaragua to overthrow the president.[8] [9] And second, the more radical of these activists or guerrilla rebels—first as part of a Junta de Reconstrucción Nacional, JRN (Junta of

---

[8] Ibid., 34.

[9] "By July 23, 1978, the Carter Administration had publicly come out against Somoza, telling the *Washington Post* 'The fact is, we're against Somoza.' " William J. Murray, *Nicaragua: Portrait of a Tragedy* (Toronto, Ontario: Mainroads Production, 1987), 30; Anastasio Somoza, *Nicaragua Betrayed* (Western Islands: 1980), 144.

National Reconstruction) and then as part of a Frente Sandinista de Liberación Nacional, FSLN[10] (Sandinista National Liberation Front) named after Augusto César Sandino, an anti-American Marxist)[11]—practiced violent means to overthrow the Somozan dynasty;[12] although, the FSLN decided not to reinstate the death penalty against the accused Somocistas (see 1977 Penal Code, Article 53). Despite the signed document stating otherwise, the Sandinistas killed government officials (not least of all—Somoza, and his political ally, Chema Castillo), while declaring that the socio-economically impoverished people of Nicaragua could either inherit wealth and power, be exiled, or face the consequence of death. In *The Black Book of Communism*, Stéphane Courtois, et al, records the "massacres, displacements of the population, and exile"[13] of the indigenous Indians of Nicaragua at the hands of the Sandinistas. This led anthropologist Gilles Bataillon "to speak of 'a politics of ethnocide' in Nicaragua."[14]

Nicaraguan revolutionary Augusto César Sandino (1895–1934). Led a rebellion for seven years between 1927–1933 against the U.S. military occupation of Nicaragua. Photo courtesy of the United States Library of Congress's Prints and Photographs division.

[10] The FSLN was created by Carlos Fonseca Amador and Tomás Borge, although they, themselves, had different political views: "Fonseca was an admirer of Castro, Borge of Mao Zedong." Stéphane Courtois, Nicolas Werth, Jean-Louis Panné, Andrzej Paczkowski, Karel Bartošek, and Jean-Louis Margolin, *The Black Book of Communism: Crimes, Terror, Repression*, trans. Jonathan Murphy and Mark Kramer (Cambridge, MA: Harvard University Press), 666.

[11] It is important to note that although these guerilla rebels were named after Sandino, they were technically not affiliated with the Sandinistas. This begs the question: why were these new Sandinistas named after Sandino? William J. Murray has this to say concerning their affiliation: "The new Sandinistas were formed in Cuba. It was the idea of Shalgadar and Fidel Castro at a brain-storming meeting of Marxist revolutionaries in Havana that the name Sandino be picked because of the folklore attached to it." Murray, *Nicaragua*, 34.

[12] The Somoza family maintained military and political control of Nicaragua for 43-years. The founder of the dynasty, Anastasio Somoza García served from 1936 to 1947 and then again from 1950 to 1956. When he was assassinated, the presidency passed to his elder son, Luis Somoza Debayle, who ruled from 1956 to 1963. His brother, Anastasio Somoza Debayle, took control from 1967 to 1972 and then again from 1974 to 1979.

[13] Courtois, *et alia, The Black Book of Communism*, 669.

[14] Ibid.

It is well known that the Sandinistas were funded and trained in Cuba, under Fidel Castro and Che Guevara's Cuban Revolution, as well as being indirectly funded by the Soviet Union, under Mikhail Gorbachev. This training in Cuba commenced in the '60s. The war officially ended on July 19, 1979, when Somoza's army surrendered. The Sandinistas—led by Daniel Ortega—celebrated that date as "The Revolution." The war left "30,000 to 50,000 people dead, a large population [600,000][15] homeless, several cities devastated by government bombing, and extensive damage to the economy, including the destruction of much of Managua's modern industrial district"[16] not including 120,000 exiled Nicaraguans.[17] Our family was fortunate enough to seek refuge in the United States.

Daniel Ortega, President of Nicaragua, February 3, 1989, during a news conference in Caracas, Venezuela. Photo courtesy of Shutterstock. By Rob Crandall.

Admittedly, the Sandinistas in the '80s initiated humanitarian efforts that positively impacted Nicaragüenses, such as a nationwide literary policy,[18] health care reforms,[19] and gender equality.[20] However, they came into international criticism for human rights abuses, such as "disappearances," prisoners who died "while attempting to escape," malnutrition, sleep deprivation, death threats, those forced to sign self-incriminating false confessions and mass executions.[21] That double standard translates to: fight for the greater good of the cause *or* we'll kill you!

While I still lived in Nicaragua, the Sandinistan manipulation tactics toward the local people were well rumored. One story I remember hearing was when a band of Sandinistas accosted a group of children for the purpose of duping them to believe that Ortega was a god. The Sandinistas would tell the poor children to pray to God in heaven to see if He would give them what they wanted. They would have the kids bow their heads at which time the children would ask God for a pair of

---

[15] Merrill, "Nicaragua," xxxi.
[16] Ibid., 73.
[17] Ibid., xxxi.
[18] Under Somoza, the illiteracy rate was 50%.
[19] For every 1,000 live births, 46 infants would die.
[20] See George Russell, "Nothing Will Stop This Revolution," *Time*, October 17, 1983, 2-3.
[21] Courtois, *et alia*, *The Black Book of Communism*, 668-74.

shoes, which never turned up under His watch. Then, they would have the kids pray to Ortega for the same thing and when they opened their eyes the Sandinistas would have ready (behind their backs) the shoes the children wanted.[22]

Fast forward to today's Sandinistas, commanded again by Ortega, they are no less shrouded in manipulation and violence. The *New York Times* recently wrote an article about how Ortega's support by his own Sandinistas is waning, while the death toll for students protesting social security reforms in Nicaragua is waxing.[23]

---

[22] In Nicaragua, Sandinistas were not officially atheists; although, it could be argued that practically speaking they were. Sandinistas were affiliated with a religious movement in Latin America known as liberation theology, which they called "Popular Church." According to Murray, "Liberation theology teaches, 'Communism is Christianity in action.' " Murray, *Nicaragua,* 50.

[23] Frances Robles, "As Nicaragua Death Toll Grows, Support for Ortega Slips," *New York Times*, May 4, 2018, https://www.nytimes.com/2018/05/04/world/americas/nicaragua-protests-ortega.html (accessed July 18, 2020).

Demonstrators protesting Nicaraguan President Daniel Ortega's visit to America outside Operation Push headquarters in Chicago, Illinois. August 2, 1986. Photo courtesy of Shutterstock. By Mark Reinstein.

Sandinistan Revolution. By Puskechina - Own work, CC BY-SA 4.0, https://commons.wikimedia.org/w/index.php?curid=63286193.

Chapter 11: *El Trompo*

My mother, Sabina Rosa Gonzalez Delagneau, dressed up at my sister and brother-in-law's home (Mildred and Luis Sevilla) in Gretna, Louisiana. 1997. She passed away three years later.

I—CHESTER—was born on December 21, 1942, in Masaya, Nicaragua, north of the capital of Managua.[24] It was the same month Enrico Fermi conducted the world's first nuclear reaction test that laid the groundwork for the first atomic bomb. My mother, Sabina Rosa Gonzalez Delagneau (born September 30, 1911; died November 1, 2000), and my father, José Delagneau Sanders (born September 5, 1905; died March 30, 1958), were born in Chontales, Nicaragua. They had five children (from eldest to youngest): Josefina Mildred, José, Rosa Lila, me and Ruby. My birth certificate reads "Chester José Delagneau Gonzalez."

---

[24] The small town of Masaya is known for its birth of two important musical instruments widely known today in Central America as maracas and marimba.

El trompo (a spinning top toy) was my favorite game to play as a child when it was just a few friends and I. But when more friends were present we played baseball on a two-acre field that my dad would rent out to the public, once a year, in honor of the patron saint Jeronimo, which featured bullfighting as the main attraction that promoted the traditional Hispanic machismo.

A photo of my father about 30-years-old. Masaya.

My father was a farmer by trade. He hired people to plant different crops, such as aniseed—a type of spice—and corn, as well as cotton, which was the big money maker. He was well-known for being a hardworking agriculturalist. As a father, I remember him as an authoritative disciplinarian with unyielding principles. He wasn't a very warm and approachable person except on the rare occasions that he drank and entertained friends on the weekends. Those are the only memories I have of him hugging me, my siblings and my mother.

On the other hand, my mom was more friendly and caring to her family. She genuinely enjoyed raising her children, which consisted of cooking for the family, making clothes for us kids and keeping a clean home. She raised us to be good Catholics and made sure that we always received the best of everything she could give or make with her own two hands.

I remained close to my mom until her death on November 1, 2000. My favorite term of endearment for her was "Lixio," which comes from her middle name, Lila. She liked to call me "Chaleoncito."

My family heritage derives from French-German roots from my father's side and Spanish roots from my mother's side. My siblings and I are third generation Nicaragüenses. My brothers and I attended an all boys' parochial school called Collegio Salesiano and my sisters attended an all girls' parochial school called Santa Teresita.

When I was about 13-years-old, my father's cotton business didn't fare well, which meant that he could no longer support the family. While we were attending school, my mother and father decided to separate in order for my father to find a way to make money, leaving my mother to raise the children. Shortly thereafter, he moved to Managua after the separation.[25] He died of pneumonia on March 30, 1957. I was 15-years-old. A couple of years later I decided to join Escuela Militar Aviacion ("Military School of Aviation") of which I remained a cadet for three years until I was sent to the United States to be trained as a pilot.

My father (about 40) and my mother (about 30). Masaya.

---

[25] My father moved in with his mistress and her children once he left our family. My mother knew about the affair that had lasted for fifteen years but, because it was so well ingrained in the culture for a married man to have sexual liaisons, she begrudgingly turned a blind eye.

Our family sans our father. Left to right: Me (4), Mildred (8), Mother (35), Rosa Lila (5) and José (6). Masaya. 1946.

Our entire family gathered together for a special occasion at my abuelita's (Luisa Sanders) home. Left to right: me (15), Father (52), Mother (46), Mildred (19), Ruby (13), José (17) and Rosa Lila (16). Managua. 1957. My father died later that year.

Chapter 12: Cadet Training

CADET TRAINING IN THE AIR FORCE IN MANAGUA consisted of aviation basics: weather navigation, aircraft (mechanical) engineering, and actual flight training in a Cessna 172 Skyhawk

followed by more advanced training in a North American Aviation T-6 Texan. Three years into the Nicaraguan Air Force Academy, I accumulated 100 hours of flight time, almost half of what is needed to graduate.

Luckily, my reputation as a skilled pilot in training caught the eye of a United States Air Force (USAF) scout commander. I was drafted as an Officer, Second Lieutenant. At that time, the USAF was known for producing the best-trained pilots in the world. Sadly, most of my Nicaraguan-trained aviation compatriots were killed for failing to receive similar proper flight training. I'm convinced that it's because I was trained in the United States that I'm alive today to tell my story.

Me at the beginning of my cadet training at the air force in Managua. November 1, 1961.

Pilot training consisted of accumulating 250 hours of flight training via visual flight route (VFR) during the day and instrument flight route (IFR) during the night, as well as being instructed in the following areas: inclement weather, acrobatic maneuvering, flight formations, cross country triangular flight routes, all the while being subjected to emergency drills from the flight commander. I was assigned one aircraft during my entire training—a North American T-28 Trojan.

After a year and a half in the United States Air Force Academy at Moody Air Force Base in Valdosta, Georgia, I graduated 4th in my class out of 30 officers. I was sent back to Nicaragua in '63 as Officer, First Lieutenant.

In Managua, I flew a wide variety of disparate aircrafts for seven years, including a North American T-6 Texan, North American T-28 Trojan, North American F-51 Mustang, Douglas C-47 Skytrain and a Martin B-26 Marauder.

Me (19) in a Titan T-51 Mustang. Managua. 1961.

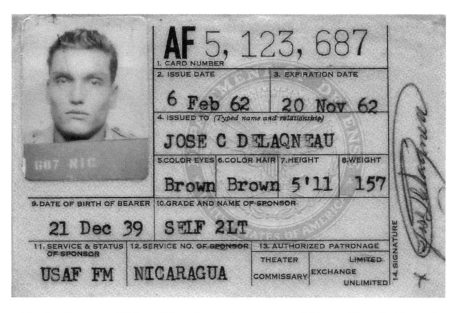

My identification and flight card for military pilot in training, Baldosta, GA. 1962. The card incorrectly reads "21 Dec 39" but I was born 21 Dec 42. I was 21-years-old.

The Cessna 172 Skyhawk is a single-engine, fixed-wing aircraft made by the Cessna Aircraft Co. No other aircraft in history is more successful than the 172 given its longevity and popularity. G-DUVL Cessna 172 Skyhawk. Photo courtesy of Rob Hodgkins.

The North American Aviation T-6 Texan was first used to train American and Royal Air Force pilots during WWII. It's arguably the greatest training aircraft ever invented; thus, earning the nickname "the pilot maker." TA-669 T-6 Texan. Photo courtesy of www.pixabay.com.

The North American T-28 Trojan is a military trainer aircraft used by the United States Air Force beginning in the 1950s. Besides being used to train pilots, it was used as a counter-insurgency aircraft during the Vietnam War. North American T-28A Trojan USAF. Photo courtesy of USAF.

The North American F-51 Mustang—a specialized fighter-bomber—was a re-designation of all P-51s in the United States Air Force (USAF) following the establishment of the USAF as a separate service. 194th Fighter Squadron. North American F-51D-30-NA Mustang 44-74607. Photo courtesy of USAF.

The Douglas C-47D Skytrain was used as a military transport workhorse by the Allies during WWII. It carried cargo and passengers, dropped paratroopers and parachuted supplies. Photo courtesy of USAF.

The United States Army Air Forces B-26 Bomber in flight. The Martin B-26 Marauder quickly received the reputation of "widowmaker" soon after entering service with the U.S. Air Force because of the early models high accident rate. Photo courtesy of USAF, http://www.maxwell.af.mil/au/afhra/photo_galleries/merhar/Photos/01097628_007.jpg.

Me (21) with my baby blue and white '57 Plymouth Fury at Moody Air Force Base, Veldosta, Georgia, after I passed the English portion of the technical aviation test at Lackland Air Force Academy. San Antonio, Texas. 1963.

USAF certificate of training completion as an undergraduate pilot from Moody Air Force Base. Veldosta, Georgia. 1963.

Me (22) at Casino Militar. President Anastasio Somoza Debayle presented me with a new rank of First Lieutenant. Managua. 1964.

Celebration after passing parachute rigger training at The School of the Americas. Left to right: me (1ˢᵗ Lt.), Roberto Amador (1ˢᵗ Lt.) and Alberto Smith (Cpt). Panama. June 15, 1967.

Chapter 13: Sitting on a Powder Keg

OUT OF ALL THE B-26 PILOTS IN '71, the air force commander chose me along with one other person to mount an airshow using real ammunition to destroy a maritime target in Lake Managua via request from Nicaraguan President Anastasio Somoza Debayle. President of Panama, Omar Torrijos, was his guest.

This happened February 1, which is known as "Nicaraguan Air Force Day." This also happened to be the auspicious day that I earned my new rank as Captain. T-33As and B-26s were used for this self-promoting aerial rally. As I said before, I flew the latter.

T-33s led the demonstration by taking off on the runway with B-26s following closely behind. In the sky, we immediately assembled in war formation strapped with six steel drums, containing fifty-five gallons of gas each. The T-33s hit the target but didn't succeed in blowing it up. But by the time the B-26s would arrive, a tremendous explosion was inevitable.

There were two B-26 bombers. Our orders were to first use our machine guns to hit the target and then individually release one 250 lb bomb to destroy any remains of it.

In the eyes of Somoza, who was sitting with other political dignitaries about one mile from the target, the aftermath was nothing short of spectacular. Admittedly, the effects of the bomb were overkill causing hundreds of thousands of dollars in collateral damage, which meant replacing shattered windows from the shock waves of the explosion that reached up to one mile from the target.

From the excitement that naturally ensued, I asked my co-pilot, Alvaro Lola, if he would humor me by performing a dangerous acrobatic maneuver known as a "barrel roll" at a very low altitude above the runway. (Such a heavy plane was not designed for acrobatics.) Reluctantly, he agreed. When we landed, Lola's concern was abated: we were received with applause from our fellow pilots, political luminaries and the president.

An USAF bomber on its way to attack Communist military targets. NARA–542247. Photo courtesy of United States National Archives and Records Administration.

Chapter 14: The Apocalypse

I WOULD LIKE TO SHIFT GEARS from discussing my surreal pilot experiences in the clouds to a monumental moment in my life on the ground. I'm talking about none other than the notorious Nicaraguan earthquake that practically leveled Managua on December 23, 1972. The country was not the same afterwards and neither were its people.

Around midnight at the Plaza Nightclub, I felt the earth move under my feet. I saw the ceiling fall to the ground killing some people instantly. Others panicked and rushed for the doors trampling each other like a herd of wildebeests. After the initial shock wore off, I conjured up the courage to get out. Immediately, I searched for an escape route. I looked to my left but I could only see bricks stacked on top of each other blocking the main entrance. Then I turned to my right. I could see a hole two feet in diameter about three-fourths up the wall. I knew that that would be my only chance of escape. So I moved a cocktail table under the hole and then jumped to freedom.

Once I was outside of the nightclub, I looked around and witnessed a tragic sight: practically every building was shaken from its foundation. I thought it was the apocalypse. Some people were walking around in a daze with dust covering their faces resembling zombies. Others fell to their knees crying over the loss of their loved ones and the devastation that was apparent all around them. I shook off this horrible sight realizing that I had to find out if my family was still alive.

I found my car in the parking lot, which was left unobstructed from the debris of the earthquake, and drove off as fast I could. Because of roadblocks, such as fires, decimated streets, and piles of dead and mutilated bodies, an excursion that should've otherwise taken fifteen minutes took over two hours. Once I got home I found that my family was safe but our home was destroyed. I did, however, find something unsettling in my bedroom.

Before the earthquake, a BTU air-conditioner weighing about 100 lb was mounted over my bed to keep the upstairs cool. But the earthquake must've shaken the unit loose causing it to come crashing down onto my bed. Had I not gone to La Plaza that night, it would've killed me.

After I assessed the damage at my place, I knew what I had to do: I had to find my girlfriend, Myriam Mendieta. So I drove frantically with the hope of holding her in my arms. White knuckling the steering wheel for over three hours, I prayed incessantly, "Oh God! Please let her be alive!"

Once I got to within 100 feet of their property, I could see the whole family standing safely in front of the house assessing the damage. "Thank you, Lord!" I sighed. There was minimal destruction to their home. I got out of my car and ran to kiss Myriam. Then we went to look for food to bring back to my family in Managua.

After we arrived back to my house, our entire family took inventory of the damage done to our home by the worst earthquake to ever hit Managua. We came to the conclusion that it was uninhabitable. Thus, we arranged to stay at our other place in the mountains for a few months. Myriam joined us. Las Nubes ("The Clouds")—a small city with a population of about 10,000 people—became our new home until our house in Managua was fully repaired.

Chapter 15: Makeshift Prison

I WAS CALLED BACK TO MILITARY SERVICE from crop-dusting cotton in Tipitapa at Juan José Somoza's farm. Little did I know that that would entail doing several things I was never trained for. I was assigned to be one of the guards at Somoza's 10-acre farm, a makeshift prison for those people arrested for looting, arson and other crimes during the earthquake. I was also in charge of food distribution at the ranch for eight months until Nicaragua started receiving relief from all around the world. The year was still 1972.

My routine as a pilot at that time included crop-dusting for six months (from July to December), for which I received Somoza's permission, and then the other six months (from January to June) I would attend to my regular duties at the air force. This routine had already been going on for six years and it would remain for another seven years. That means that from '66 to '79 I worked as both a crop-duster and an air force pilot.[26]

By the end of '72, Myriam and I were dating each other exclusively. In March—Myriam's birthday month—we were elated to find out that we were having a baby.

After the devastation of the earthquake came something new, something good—life! A child was to be born into the world, and he was ours. No grief from any natural disaster would change how we felt about being soon-to-be-parents. With this child came hope, hope of a new life for us all. As summer approached, I knew I'd have to reluctantly leave my family, on a daily basis, to complete my duties as a crop-duster.

My routine began with me getting up at 3:30 a.m. every morning for six months throughout the year. Each night, Myriam would prepare a small breakfast for me that I ate on the way to work in my olive-green Buick Electra. I'd be on the road by 4 a.m. in order to arrive in Tipitapa an hour later. Once I got to the plantation—El Triunfo—it took me about an hour to prepare the plane filling it with gas and pesticides for the crops. By 6 a.m. the sun began to rise with all its glory affording me visibility to spray. It was important to start early—at the first sign of sunlight—before the wind picks up tossing the discharged poison to and fro.

This routine didn't pose a problem for me except when it interfered with me being present at my first child's birth. One would think that calling in sick or asking for a personal day at work would be acceptable, but things worked differently for my line of work. If I didn't fumigate the day's allotment of cotton, the crop could've been seriously damaged leaving the owner seriously dissatisfied and me seriously unemployed.[27] So I had to work come hell or high water, seven days a week, six months straight to help my family rebuild our home in Managua. At this time, I also started saving up to build a new house for my new family in Casa Colorada.

---

[26] I worked as a crop-duster to supplement our family's income. Working as an air force pilot for the Nica Air Force paid peanuts compared to what I earned as a seasonal crop-duster. In one month, I earned $15,000 crop-dusting. Piloting I earned $200 monthly.

[27] I remember a time when I had a high fever and I was supposed to fumigate a large crop. If I didn't work, the owner of the plantation would've taken a big hit, financially. So I did whatever I had to do in order to work. In this particular situation, I inserted a rectal suppository until my fever broke.

Chapter 16: "Chestercito"

OUR FIRST CHILD—Chester José Delagneau, Jr. ("Chestercito")—was born on October 15, 1973 weighing 6 lb, 13 oz in a Baptist hospital in Managua.[28] Myriam was in labor for 16 hours but Chestercito never "crowned." So Myriam had our first son via cesarean section at 9 a.m.

I arrived shortly after crop-dusting to celebrate my son's birth, but I was unable to hold him because he was immediately whisked away into an incubator. But I did get to hold a cup of Champagne and share a toast with the doctor (Uriel Martinez) and the attending nurse. Myriam was not discharged from the hospital until three days later on account of her C-section. At that time, we returned home to Casa Colorada.

We prepared a bassinet for Chestercito in our room wanting him close to us in case of any emergencies. Soon following, we hired a full-time nanny to help Myriam with some of the childcare responsibilities of being a first-time mommy.

One month after Chestercito was born. Casa Colorada. November 1973.

---

[28] I chose a Baptist hospital for the birth of our son because Baptist hospitals were famed as being the best hospitals at the time.

Chestercito's first birthday. Myriam's seamstress sowed a pilot uniform for Jr. Casa Colorada. 1974.

Left to right: Luis ("Lucho") Sevilla, Chestercito (1), my sister, Mildred, and my brother's first wife, Damaris, in our living room. Casa Colorada. 1974.

Myriam (23) with Chestercito (1) in the garden of our home. Casa Colorada. Christmas 1974.

Chestercito (almost 2). Casa Colorada. 1975.

Chestercito's 4th birthday wearing a military jumpsuit that was made especially for him. He's toting his favorite teddy bear and wheeled-horsy. Las Colinas Sur. 1977.

Chapter 17: Playas de Pochomil

FAMILY would come to visit during the weekends. We would caravan together to the beach on Fridays and return on Sundays to unload our belongings and mentally prepare for the following workweek. Actually, we frequented the same beach—Playas de Pochomil—every time because of the special attention we received from the hotel owners. The hotel, made of bamboo, sat right on the beach. Matter of fact, at high tide, the water would stretch its frothy fingers to claw at the thick bamboo columns that held up the roof. Pochomil had about 10 rooms measuring 100 square feet each. The roof consisted of sheets of aluminum siding overlapping one another. The wall's infrastructure was made of intertwined bamboo with Palm branches decorating the interior. And just in case the guests of the hotel forgot where they were, the owners made sure to remind them by leaving beach sand on the floor of each room along with a cozy hammock tied to two bamboo poles inserted deep into the earth.

A Saturday morning at Pochomil started early. After a quick breakfast that consisted of eggs, *gallopinto* (fried rice and beans), boiled plantains, and *pinolillo* (cornmeal and cacao-based drink), we were escorted by the owners of the hotel down the dark sandy beach to Las Rocas at low tide so that the children could enjoy catching baby crabs in the tide pools. The adults went to barter with the fishermen over the catch of the day. The fish then were taken back to the hotel to be prepared for lunch. After lunch we either took a siesta or we talked about the rest of the day's itinerary, which typically consisted of going horseback riding, swimming in the Pacific Ocean, playing Frisbee and/or flying a kite. At night my uncle Federico Gonzalez would tell "ghost stories" by a fire on the beach about El Cadejo,[29] which everyone loved to hear. On Sundays, we stayed with the same schedule as the previous day until 2 p.m. when we packed up our belongings to return home.

Chestercito (6-months-old). Playas de Pochomil. April 1974.

---

[29] El Cadejo is Nicaraguan folklore about an evil shaggy dog with flaming red eyes that walked upright on its skinny legs attached to goat's hooves. It would appear to people who were out after midnight.

Chapter 18: Surviving the Angel of Death

IN 1974, several significant events transpired—two of which ended with people losing their lives while flying. There is a tradition for Spanish and Latin countries to celebrate a *verbena* (country fair) during the summer, usually during the month of August following the Santo Domingo festivities. Nicaragua has participated in this fair for many years. That year, Mexico decided to participate in Nicaragua's national fair by sending 24 Mexican children to sing Mexican-style music.

On Friday morning, the children were to board at Mexico's capital onto a military C-47 that Somoza authorized. The Chief of Operations of Flying (COF) notified two pilots that they would be scheduled to pick up the children at Distrito Federal (Mexico City). Fabio Molina and I were the two pilots chosen. But two days before takeoff, I fell ill and went to see the military doctor. He told me I was not healthy to fly and thus I ended up not being able to pick up the kids. The COF replaced me with another pilot, Lt. Bravo.

Once the scheduled date arrived, Molina and Bravo picked up their precious cargo and flew back to Nicaragua so the children could participate in the verbena that same evening. The plane was scheduled to arrive at four o'clock but due to a tumultuous storm covering Guatemala, El Salvador and Nicaragua, the plane failed to arrive.[30] It wasn't until later that night that we received news that the airplane carrying the 24 children crashed into the Pacific Ocean, near Tamarindo, El Salvador, killing every person onboard, including two pilots and a flight engineer. What a tragedy!

Later that same year God spared my life yet again when I was called off a military training assignment. I was putting on my parachute to fly a B-26 Bomber with Henry Muñoz, a major in the Nicaraguan Air Force, who requested my presence on this routine aviation since I had a plethora of experience flying B-26s. Just as I was about to enter the runway, the COF—Luis Lopez—made us turn off the engines. He approached the airplane to tell me he was going to replace me on the flight. Because he was my superior, I acquiesced.

I climbed out and he climbed in. As I stayed on the ground I watched the airplane take off. Typically, during "take off," a plane climbs about 1,000 feet per minute reaching at least 9,000 feet. But in this case, it never ascended above 700 feet. The grounds-men and I knew something was wrong because the plane was circumnavigating the runway. And that's when we saw smoke coming out of the right engine. Muñoz and Lopez tried to land the plane, but it stalled. Suddenly, they went in to a nosedive and smashed onto the ground. The airplane exploded killing both men on impact.

---

[30] En route, over Guatemalan skies, Captain Molina radioed his air force commander asking permission to land in Guatemala since he was no longer able to control the airplane on account of the storm. The commander denied his request barking at him to arrive on time.

Chapter 19: "You May Kiss the Bride!"

THAT SAME YEAR ('74), we decided to move from our home in Casa Colorada to live in my sister's house that was in another town called Barrio Largaespada. My sister and her husband—Mildred and Luis ("Lucho") Sevilla—had moved to the United States for a year, so they let us use their *quinta* (house) during that time. A year later, after some of the devastation of the earthquake began to subside from our memories, we decided it was the right time to get married.

On December 31, 1974, we replaced painful memories of loss and brokenness with joyful memories of belonging and wholeness. We were married in the presence of Pastora ("Pastorcita") and Danilos Sanchez at their home in Managua.[31]

Then in '75, I purchased some land on which to build our future home in an affluent neighborhood, called Las Colinas Sur, Managua. I had my brother, José Delagneau Gonzalez, who was a civil engineer at the time, construct the blueprints of the house. He then contracted out the building of it that began construction by late '76 and was quasi finished by late '77. During this time, God blessed us yet again!

---

[31] We enjoyed a simple wedding. About 10 people were in attendance. The ceremony was scheduled for midnight in order to bring the joy of our union into the New Year. Pictures were taken to commemorate this special day. But due to the urgency of our departure vis-à-vis The Revolution, we were unable to take these priceless photos with us to America. The photos that were left behind were destroyed by the Sandinistas.

Chester De Lagneau — **December 31st** — **Myriam Mendietta**

France — **1974** — **Spain**

© The Historical Research Center 1996

French Crest: Meaning of the family name: "(son) of the Lamb." Symbolism: The white (or silver) color represents purity, innocence, beauty and gentleness. The blue color represents truth and loyalty. And the gold color represents generosity and elevation of mind. The chevron stands for protection. The lamb symbolizes gentleness and patience under suffering. The white roses signify love and faith.

Spanish Crest: Meaning of the family name: The family name was derived from the place where the ancestral home was located. Symbolism: The white (or silver) color represents purity, innocence, beauty and gentleness. The blue color represents truth and loyalty. The red color signifies the qualities of military strength and nobility and fairness. And the gold color represents generosity and elevation of mind. The canton (borne at the top corner of the shield) was a reward from the sovereign for performance of eminent service. The chief (horizontal band across the top of the shield) was granted as a special reward for prudence and wisdom or successful military command. The crescent moon means hope and joy. The fleur-de-lis stands for purity and light. The tree denotes the bearing of fruit. The two mullets (five pointed stars) represent a knight's spur, which means divine quality from above. The lion rampant (upright) stands for fairness and nobility.

This picture of the Delagneau and Mendietta family crests is used with permission from the Historical Research Center (HRC).

Chapter 20: "Born-Again" Christian

I—MYRIAM—BECAME A "BORN-AGAIN" CHRISTIAN in the summer of '76. But it didn't happen by chance. A few years earlier, I'd met a poor, elderly woman, named Doña Victoria, who was the caretaker of a Baptist church that was at the entrance of our town called Casa Colorada.[32] I would occasionally take seasonal vegetables, such as radishes and carrots, to her church. Not long after, we started a friendship that blossomed into a mentoring relationship. She would often come over to my house to talk when Chester would be out fumigating. I remember one conversation we had when she said that she felt unworthy to be eating at my table. I responded back by saying, "Don't feel that way. You're a child of God. You're wise and you serve Him humbly, better than I." That relationship planted a seed in my heart—a seed of desire, desire to draw closer to God.

From that day forward, I began listening to a Spanish speaking American evangelist on the radio. Reverend David Spencer was his name. It was on that station, called Ondas de Luz ("Wave of Light"), that I learned that Managua was to have a Christian crusade that summer ('76). Famous Argentinian Pastor, Luis Palou, was going to be the main speaker.

On Friday night, I went to the crusade by myself since Chester was working for the air force. Indicative of evangelical crusades, it was held in a sizeable tent with loads of worship music. People were lifting their hands and dancing in the aisles, as they sang their hearts out to the Lord. Pastor Palou gave what's called an "altar call"—that's when people come up to the altar to respond to the salvation message by becoming a "born-again" Christian. I immediately went up to the front. To my surprise, I saw my mother at the altar worshipping intently. Once I got her attention, we hugged and cried in each other's arms.

I left with joy and hope knowing that my life from this point forward would be forever different, now that I have my own personal relationship with the Lord, a relationship with the Lord that was fostered by my own spiritual mentor, Doña Victoria.

---

[32] Besides being a place of comfort and support for me after the earthquake, Casa Colorada was a beautiful community of 500 houses at a high elevation of about 2,500 feet above sea level. It was a breezy, yet charming town with its very own bakery, farmer's market and restaurant-motel (El Capri) that was only half and hour away from the beach at Masachapa.

Chapter 21: Chester Lassos Stork Again

IN OCTOBER OF '76, we discovered that Myriam was pregnant again with another boy. Jean Pierre "JP" Delagneau was born via C-section on June 7, 1977, weighing the size of a small turkey—10 lb—that morning in a military hospital. Chestercito was already 3½-years-old when JP was born.

The boys slept in their own bedrooms except, I remember, JP slept in a basinet in our room until he was 2-months-old. When we moved into our new home in Las Colinas Sur with two beautiful, healthy boys the construction of our house was not entirely complete. And because of the civil war that had begun in '77 and would last until '79 with the Sandinistas holding dominant political and military power in Nicaragua until '90, our home would never be completed.

Myriam (26) holding our beautiful newborn baby boy, JP, with Chestercito (3½) by their side in our living room. Las Colinas Sur. June 19, 1977.

Myriam (26), Chestercito (4) and JP (almost 1) at Galeria Del Arte: Estudios Fotographicos. Managua. 1977.

Me (almost 36) and my boys, Chestercito (4) and JP (almost 1) sitting on my lap in my rocking chair in the living room. Myriam and I purchased a his-and-her set of rocking chairs in Masaya. Las Colinas Sur. 1978.

El Pequeño Vaquero ("The Little Cowboy"), JP (1)
at Galeria Del Arte: Estudios Fotographicos.
Managua. 1978.

JP won the grand prize of $100 (mil córdobas) and a round trip ticket to Miami
(for Mama) for a photo contest sponsored by Galeria Del Arte as the most
photogenic child one month before his first birthday. Managua. 1978.

JP (almost 1) and Chestercito (4). To the right of this picture was a working waterfall that practically made up the entire wall of the dinning room. On the rocks hung several water plants that Myriam made room for. Las Colinas Sur. 1978.

JP's first birthday. Myriam's seamstress sowed JP's sailor suit, as well as the dress she's wearing in the picture. Las Colinas Sur. June 7, 1978.

Chapter 22: Bona-Fide Civil War

AS I MENTIONED BEFORE, the civil war in Nicaragua started in '77. It was an insurgency by the communist Sandinistas inciting the poor people's help to fight the Somozan military regime.[33] (In this section, my intention is not necessarily to give a history lesson of the infamous war in Nicaragua, but to give a personal account of the war from memory. I seek to explain my experiences during the war that changed the course of the lives of our family forever. With that said, however, I will preface my story with some historical facts that set up my involvement in the war.)

Early 1970s, La Guardia or the Nicaraguan National Guard under the dictatorship of Anastasio Somoza Debayle, went into high alert when guerilla rebels trained in Cuba ambushed and killed Somozan guards in the northern mountainous jungle near Honduras. Each pueblo in Nicaragua had its own guards that made up the whole of La Guardia. The alert also affected civilians who were restricted via Marshall Law from leaving their homes after 8 p.m. The country was virtually locked down and for good reason.

After the ambush in the North, the guerillas usurped power over three important geographical locations in Nicaragua prior to the devastating earthquake that hit Managua in '72. Palacio National was the most important conquest because that's where 400 to 500 government officials worked. (The other two locations were La Calle Rusbel that led from Lake Managua to Somoza's palace and La Casa de Chema Castillo, where Castillo—political ally with Somoza—was assassinated.) Psychologically, this put the people of Nicaragua in a state of anxiety seeing that the guerillas were now a real threat to Somoza's guards. La Guardia's return-fire was hardly affective in causing the communist rebels to retreat. The Nicaraguan Air Force was minimally involved at this embryonic point in the war with one helicopter patrolling the insurgency and relaying information to La Guardia. It wasn't until a few years later that the air force became active in what became a bona-fide civil war.[34]

One important event that electrified the war efforts of the Sandinistas, as well as inciting opposition against Somoza by formerly unspoken Nicaraguan proletariat and bourgeoisie, was the 1978 assassination of Pedro Joaquín Chamorro, a well-respected editor-and-chief of the liberal

---

[33] It's important to note that if it were not for the aid of communist countries, such as Russia and Cuba, the Sandinistan uprising would most likely have never been successful.

It's also of importance to remember that Cuba was quick to provide aid to Nicaraguan insurgents because Somoza's administration cooperated with the United States to allow Americans to train Batista-loyalist Cuban pilots on Nicaraguan soil in Puerto Cabeza. The Bay of Pigs Invasion (1961)—the failed US military invasion of communist Cuba with the aid of eight B-26 bombers—left Nicaragua to bomb Cuba. Helping to overthrow an anti-Cuban Nicaraguan government became Fidel Castro's personal vendetta.

The failed invasion strengthened Castro's leadership immortalizing his position and making him a national hero. It also led to the Cuban Missile Crisis (1962) reinforcing relations between Cuba and the Soviet Union.

[34] This was not because the air force was reluctant to go to war. Jet planes carrying bombs can cause colossal collateral damage. Combine this with the fact that the opposition was defined by its guerilla tactics that made them extremely difficult to locate, and you have a war that is better fought on the ground if the government seeks to keep the casualty count down.

newspaper La Prensa, who was overtly Anti-Somozan. The Nicaraguan people loved Chamorro because he was not afraid to publish the truth about Somoza's political practices, as well as his personal *faux pas*. So, once the Nicaragüenses heard of this injustice, it fueled the fire of insurrection against Somoza since the people assumed that the president had funded this heinous act. It's well-known that Chamorro was murdered by Silvio Pena Rivas, who admitted to being paid $14,300 by Dr. Pedro Ramos, a Cuban-American, to assassinate the editor.[35] However, what is not well-know is that Rivas and his father played both sides of the political struggle between Somicistas and Sandinistas, and thus, as a mercenary, Rivas took advantage of the sensitive situation by siding with the highest bidder.

In my opinion, the intentional killing of Chamorro, who was outspokenly against Somoza, was the strategic political tactic by the Sandinistas to set up Somoza as the culprit, not least of all because the president would receive the most backlash from the people. I was not a Somocista, although, I was a Contra (contra-revolutionary) or freedom fighter. However, I don't believe Somoza would've had Chamorro murdered during a time when everyone would've suspected it. As I mentioned earlier, the editor of La Prensa was a highly esteemed man—to the point of being a national hero—because he was an honest journalist who believed in printing the truth about everyone and everything. Despite the turbulent socio-political times, Chamorro did not carry a firearm, believing the people's support protected him from the government's threat.

As the war intensified and reached its zenith in '79, I found myself as an air force major feeling hopeless about winning the war against the Sandinistas. I was placed second in command of operations by the chief of operations, Marcial Lopez, who took military orders from the air force commander, Orlando Zeledon, who in turn took military orders from Anastasio Somoza Debayle, commander-in-chief of the military.

My military duties consisted of sending out airplanes carrying a troop of 30 men at a time armed with grenades, M-16s, and bazookas to strategic airstrips in the north near Honduras. I was also in charge of organizing the return of aircrafts carrying wounded and dead soldiers loyal to Somoza.

Boys as young as 16-years-old, mostly illiterate, volunteered to fight in La Guardia. Each pueblo had its own commando—typically ill trained, out of shape seniors—who trained these juvenile country bumpkins. Because this outfit was ill prepared to fight against the insurgents, a more sophisticated military training was formed by Somoza. The new convoy was called Escuela de Entrenamiento Basico de Infanteria (EEBI).

To be accepted into EEBI, military prospects had to have a primary education and be between the ages of 16 to 20. But even this new and improved military outfit was no match for the evasive guerillas trained by a communist powerhouse like Cuba. In the span of five and a half months—from February to mid July—I saw hundreds of wounded and dead EEBI graduates being shipped

---

[35] Riding, "Murder of Anti-Somoza Newsman Has Deepened Crisis in Nicaragua," 2.

back in C-47s. I was responsible for calling the hospital to arrange for transportation of the dead and wounded.[36]

I clearly remember shaking these *razos's*—graduates of basic training—hands just before they were deployed to Ocotal, Puerto Cabeza, San Carlos, León and Chinandega. Armed with M-16s and belts of bullets held together by fit physiques, they seemed so optimistic about participating in the brutalities of war and confident of their presumed omnipotence and immortality, which is typical of being young and foolish. As anyone who's shed blood in battle knows, nothing humbles one's ego and silences pride like death. I cannot begin to speak of the horrors I witnessed during this time of civil unrest. A deep depression gripped me around the throat when I saw these young men as they returned from the fight, but this time they lay stiffly in body bags riddled with bullet holes and missing limbs. The look of invulnerability was drained from their blue faces.

---

[36] There was only one military hospital for all the soldiers returning from war—either dead or alive—in Managua in '79.

Chapter 23: "We Can't Win!"

ON JULY 9, 1979, I realized that winning the war against the Sandinistas was lost. I received my last air load of soldiers, the majority of whom were dead captains and majors—some of whom were my closest friends. The few soldiers who were still alive, although wounded, were their subordinates. They spoke like the Israelite spies who'd just returned from exploring the land of Canaan during the time of Moses saying, "They were like 500 and we were only 50. We can't win!"

That day was an especially bittersweet day for me. In the afternoon, Col. Enrique Bermudez landed at the air force base where I was receiving the dead and wounded. He told me that Somoza was leaving, although, Somoza had assured everyone in the military that he would never be deposed. Col. Bermudez confided in me that when Somoza leaves, he would become the commander-in-chief of the military, and I would be promoted to air force commander. I felt honored but disturbed at the same time. Because I was receiving the news of what was happening on the front lines as it came in—moment by moment—I knew that staying to lead the air force against the Sandinistas would be a lost cause.

Chapter 24: La Nica Airlines

I WENT TO SOMOZA TO ASK PERMISSION TO LEAVE NICARAGUA on July 11, 1979. I told him it was a necessary trip to the United States of America to see a doctor about my heart condition. Truth be told: I never had a heart condition. I wanted more than anything to be joined with my wife and sons, to hold them again. He told me I had five days and then I had to return. I remember thinking *I only need one day*—because I wasn't coming back. But just in case Somoza negated my request, I spotted a twin engine Aero Commander full of fuel that was headed to Costa Rica. Ultimately, I gave the permission memorandum to leave the country to the general manager of La Nica Airlines who made me buy a round trip ticket to Miami, Florida; however, I secretly knew that I only need a one-way ticket.

Looking back, I realize that it was divine Providence that led me to talk to Somoza. On June 16, 1979, almost a month prior, I'd sent my wife and children out of the country with my mother, sister and her husband—Rosa Lila, Mildred and Lucho—to seek asylum in the United States to live with my sister's (Rosa Lila) family in New Orleans, Louisiana. But before they could get there they would all need to have new passports issued and sent to them in Honduras where they remained stranded waiting anxiously for them to arrive. Before Myriam left with our kids, she gave me a copy of the Bible in Spanish. I faithfully read the Psalter, especially Psalms 23 and 91; they became my constant companions.

After I was told I could leave, I packed a change of clothes and some personal belongings and left at 3 p.m. the next day, July 12, on La Nica Airlines.[37] The connecting flight into New Orleans did not leave Miami until 7 a.m. the next day. I got into New Orleans International Airport on July 13th at 9 a.m. where my wife, brother, José, and brothers-in-law, Edwin ("Eddie") Blais and Martin Hinzie, met me.

As I think back to the day I left Nicaragua, I see God's hand of protection over my life. I had my father-in-law, Santiago Juncadela, drive me to the airport around 1 p.m. in my green '72 Ford Fairlane. I left the car with him, which he drove back to his house. I found out later by my mother-in-law that the Sandinistas had first searched our house and then Santiago's, seeking to kill me. As it turned out, one of the Sandinistas present was a "friend" of ours who used to wait on us at El Club de Las Colinas (Las Colinas Club), which we frequented often with the kids and their nanny, Lourdes. We did not know he was a Sandinista at the time, although, he knew full well that I was part of Somoza's Guardia. He even asked me to be his son's godfather, but I turned him down,

---

[37] At this point it's important to note that when I left Nicaragua, I left behind our most valuable personal belongings. (In seven days, the insurgency would completely eclipse the Somozan government. The 50-year Somozan dynasty would come to an end via Sandinistan guerillas on July 19, 1979. On that day, American President Jimmy Carter gave Anastasio Somoza Debayle and his cabinet political asylum.) Because of the war, we lost ownership of our four homes—the sum of which came to three quarters of a million (American) dollars. And because the bank was closed the day of my departure due to economic instability, I couldn't retrieve our savings, which totaled $100,000. I had to borrow money (about $600) from my mother-in-law, Doña Julia, to buy a plane ticket out of Nicaragua.

thanks to Lourdes, who'd cautioned me to be careful about the situation. The communist guerillas were setting traps for the men of the military and their families in order to torture and assassinate them.

Providentially, God saw me out of the corner of His eye. Although I can say this with certainty now, it was not until I was joined with my family in Louisiana, attending a non-denominational charismatic church, that I put my trust in Jesus Christ as my own personal Lord, Savior, King and Commander-in-Chief of my life.

This is the last picture Myriam and I took together before we left Nicaragua. My big brother, José, took the photo. Masachapa. February 3, 1979.

PART II
Louisiana

Chapter 1: New Orleans International Airport

WITH ONLY TWO SUITCASES—one for the boys and the other for me—we made it out of Nicaragua just in time. Everyone leaving the country was seeking asylum in either Honduras or Costa Rica. We chose Tegucigalpa, Honduras.

The flight to Tegucigalpa was especially turbulent. Chester arranged for a private airplane that seated 12 passengers to fly 9 of us—Chestercito, JP, Chester's mother (Rosa Lila), Mildred, Lucho, me and three strangers—out of Nicaragua. The pilot, Fernando Ocón, was highly skilled in flying this particular aircraft. The problem, however, was twofold: the low clinging clouds and the mountainous topography presented a substantial challenge to even the most experienced pilots.

Later I asked Chester why the plane frequently banked to the left and then to the right, dipping its wings 90 degrees each time, while there were—what's technically called—"convective currents" (ascending and descending air movements) that dropped and raised the plane between 500–1000 feet. He explained to me that a phenomenon of air occurs between mountains. The wind typically scales up the face of one mountain to circle around and thus scale down the side of the adjacent mountain. This caused a powerful whirlwind to toss our small aircraft back and forth and up and down. No wonder my boys and I were terrified. I thank God that the flight to Tegucigalpa was only an hour long.

When we finally arrived, every hotel was booked with a waiting list due to the flood of immigrants to Honduras. The only thing we could find was a hostel.

Meanwhile, Chester continued to look for our passports. During the socio-political upheaval caused by the war, no one was distributing passports at the federal building. So Chester hired two men to help him look through a volcano of about 80,000 passports to find ours. It took them two days to successfully locate the proper paperwork, which Chester sent as priority mail to us. Upon receiving them, we immediately booked a flight with TACA Airlines.

The plane ride from Tegucigalpa to New Orleans was also rough. My youngest son, Jean Pierre, who'd just turned 2-years-old, wouldn't stop crying, partially due to an ear infection. Add to that the emotional turmoil of losing our homes, being torn apart from my mother and sisters and not knowing if I would ever see my husband again who was mandated to stay and fight as a Contra in the war.

From the time it took to book a flight to New Orleans and arrive at the New Orleans International Airport, three days had passed. We got in around 4 p.m.

On June 28, 1979, Chester's brother, José, his sister, Rosa Lila, and her husband, Eddie, met us at the airport. We piled into Eddie's brown '78 Ford LTD Landau and José's white '69 Ford Mustang, heading to Eddie's home in Algiers to celebrate our arrival. The boys and I stayed with the Blais's (Rosa Lila, Eddie and their two children, Jared and Leslie) in New Orleans, on the West Bank of the Mississippi River, until Chester arrived about a month later.[38]

We are forever grateful for the love, support and hospitality that the Blais's showed us during this challenging time of acclimating our family to a new reality.

On the front porch of Eddie's home—206 Neil Avenue—shortly after our arrival sans Chester. Left to right: Carolina Gonzalez (Chester's 1st cousin), Chestercito, Leslie, Ruby ("Tootie") and Damarita holding JP. New Orleans. June 1979.

---

[38] I remember that a week before Chester met up with us, a reporter for the local newspaper came to Eddie's home to interview all of us regarding the situation in Nicaragua that deracinated us from our familial roots.

Chapter 2: "An Act of Barbarism"

ON JUNE 20, 1979, the *New York Times* headline read, "ABC Reporter and Aide Killed By Soldier in Nicaraguan Capital." American journalist Bill Stewart was assassinated point blank by a Somozan guard. This act of terrorism was broadcast all over the world. The following day, U.S. President, Jimmy Carter, addressed the nation on live television saying that he would not tolerate such "an act of barbarism that all civilized people condemn."[39] He immediately withdrew all aid to the Somozan government. (Some believe La Guardia wasn't responsible for the American news correspondent's assassination, but rather a Sandinistan rebel dressed in Nicaraguan National Guard uniform in order to incite hatred for Somoza and everything he represented.) After Carter had personally granted Somoza political asylum into the United States, he reneged his promise and exiled Somoza.[40]

---

[39] The American Presidency Project, "Jimmy Carter, Bill Stewart Statement on the Death of the ABC News Correspondent," Online by Gerhard Peters and John T. Woollley, June 21, 1979, https://www.presidency.ucsb.edu/documents/bill-stewart-statement-the-death-the-abc-news-correspondent (accessed July 18, 2020).

[40] Somoza then sought asylum in Paraguay under then dictator Alfredo Stroessner. While in Paraguay, Somoza was assassinated on September 17, 1980 after he had resigned. He was ambushed and killed by a Sandinistan commando team.

Chapter 3: "Out of Harm's Way"

I ARRIVED INTO THE UNITED STATES on July 13, 1979, no doubt due to the persistent prayers of my family, friends and even strangers who attended Rosa Lila's church and Ruby's church. My family warmly greeted me at the airport. I was overwhelmed with joy at seeing my wife who I didn't know if I'd ever see again. It had been over three weeks, which felt like a lifetime since I'd seen her. Needless to say, when we met again, I held onto her with the surreal feeling that we were finally reunited and out of harm's way.

Shortly after arriving at Eddie's home, the rest of my relatives showered me with much needed affection. We ate, talked, laughed, cried and then we did it all over again. I was emotionally overwhelmed to say the least. (I could take this time to tell you what it was like to hug and kiss my boys again, but no amount of words could ever fully describe the concentrated love I felt in my heart toward them.)

As we ate Chinese food and discussed the details of my escape, the promises of Psalm 23 and Psalm 91 flooded my mind: "Even though I walk through the darkest valley, I will fear no evil" and "Do not be afraid of the terrors of the night, nor the arrow that flies in the day . . . If you make the LORD your refuge . . . no evil will conquer you. . ." That night—sharing about God's presence, protection and faithfulness over me—will forever burn in my memory as brightly as the sun.

My brother, José, invited us to stay with him, his wife (Damaris) and their children (José René and Damarita) in Gretna, Louisiana, awhile. That while turned into a year.

My first day reunited with my family at Eddie's house. New Orleans. July 13, 1979.

When I returned, I didn't want to be away from Myriam for a single second. New Orleans.
July 13, 1979.

When I returned, Chestercito wanted to be next to me all night. New Orleans. July 13, 1979.

Group photo of the Blais's with Chestercito the day I arrived from Nicaragua. Left to right: (back) Rosa Lila, Eddie and Jared; (front) Chestercito and Leslie. New Orleans. July 13, 1979.

The French Quarter Fountain in Jackson Square in front of St. Louis Cathedral a few months after I met up with my family in Louisiana. New Orleans. Fall 1979.

Around the time we moved-in with my brother and his family. Left to right: Myriam, Damarita and Damaris, and in the bottom right corner, Chestercito. Gretna. Fall 1979.

In front of my brother's house. Left to right: Myriam, Chestercito and Damarita. Gretna. Fall 1980.

Chapter 4: *Nacatamales*

I—MYRIAM—PRAYED TO GOD TO GIVE ME WISDOM in order to help my family make money during the time we stayed with José and his family. As I read the Bible, I came across Psalm 90:17: "Let the favor of the Lord our God be upon us, and establish the work of our hands upon us; yes, establish the work of our hands!" (ESV) So I started working with my hands making *nacatamales*. My best clients were those people I'd contacted through the Yellow Pages. I'd looked up Spanish last names and cold-called them. When the people asked me how I got their phone number, I told them that my family and I came from Nicaragua as refugees and I make delicious *nacatamales* that are different from the typical tamales made from corn *masa*.

Later, when we were living in New Orleans, I contacted a local supermarket called La Union and told them of my special tamales. The owner tried one and loved it. He began giving out samples and, before I knew it, La Union was carrying my *nacatamales* in their refrigerated shelves.

What makes my *nacatamales* so special is that I borrow from the typical Nicaraguan *nacatamale* recipe, which requires only potato *masa*, yet I use both corn *masa*, which is typical of Mexican tamales, as well as potato *masa* giving it a thicker, firmer feel. My *nacatamales* include pork, rice, tomatoes, capers, green olives, cocktail onions, prunes, and other tasty ingredients.

After I've hand wrapped each *nacatamale* in banana leaves, waxed paper, and aluminum foil to hold in the flavor, I boil them in water. Each *nacatamale* weighs over a pound. This divinely inspired dish has become a traditional Christmas breakfast on Christmas Day for the Delagneaus—honoring God's faithfulness to our family.

Words cannot express how appreciative we are for the kindness we received from my brother-in-law and his family for taking us into their home. At the time, we could only borrow to survive; we weren't in any position to give back. We can say with all confidence that our family has always been there for us.

My famous *nacatamale.*

Chapter 5: Asylum

I—CHESTER—APPLIED FOR ASYLUM AROUND THIS TIME. (Asylum in the United States for one of Somoza's military guards, as I once was, meant that I would not be forced to return to Nicaragua where the Sandinistas were waiting to kill all former refugees.)[41] I was personally told by a U.S. immigration officer that as soon as the civil war was over my family and I would be deported back to Nicaragua. That of course would ensure our death sentence. Although I was verbally denied asylum, I still applied.

After a month, I checked in with the immigration department. Mysteriously, they had no record of my application. I then decided to reapply. Shortly thereafter, I was informed that there was a law on the books that allowed refugees to receive residency—without having been first granted asylum— by having a sibling, who is a U.S. citizen, request to have his/her brother/sister become a resident of the United States. My sister, Rosa Lila Blais, did just that for me. And, of course, if I were granted residency then my wife and children would automatically receive residency.

About two years after we applied, while living in New Orleans (2942 De Soto Street), we became residents of the United States. This meant that we would not be deported back to Nicaragua where we would all be assassinated. The moment we received news of the event that would change our lives forever, we cried. We then prayed and then cried some more. That same day we made a reservation for later that evening to celebrate at our favorite restaurant on Bourbon Street called Houlihan's Restaurant and Bar.

---

[41] The sooner I received asylum the closer I was to receive residency; and the sooner I received residency the closer I was to receive citizenship.

Our California family—the Pinell's—came to visit us. In front of the French Quarter Fountain in Jackson Square. Left to right: (back) Alex Jr. and Chestercito, (front) Yolanda, José, Damaris, Myriam, Damarita, me and JP. New Orleans. 1980.

Chapter 6: The Pitfalls of the Word-Faith Movement

CHIMBA AND ROSA LILA INVITED US TO ATTEND THEIR CHARISMATIC CHURCH in Metairie. Coming from a Catholic background in Nicaragua where hardly any emotions were expressed, a charismatic non-denominational church was an exciting place to spend Sunday mornings. Our need for security after surviving a devastating earthquake and an even deadlier civil war was met by our spiritual brothers and sisters in the Lord; they reminded us of God's miracles and promises that brought us into their parish. We were emotionally nurtured and spiritually fed a consistent doctrine of the Holy Spirit and His power indwelling us *if* only we would believe.

It was at this church that I placed my faith in Jesus Christ as my personal Lord and Savior. I was also encouraged to be baptized in the Holy Spirit being assured that the same Spirit that indwelt Christ at His incarnation and resurrection dwelt also in me. Thus, the same power Christ wielded by the Spirit to heal the sick and raise the dead was also living in me. There were no limitations that could be put on me except the ones that I put on myself. Whatever I spoke by faith in the spiritual realm would manifest in the physical realm. Thus, if someone needed prayer it was my responsibility to pray for him/her, so s/he could receive whatever s/he asked for—be it monetary or spiritual.

"Nothing is impossible for God," went the mantra. And if I'd prayed in faith for a person and s/he did not receive an answer to prayer, then it was his/her lack of faith that prohibited God from answering. Thus, there was no need for medicine or doctors. To seek medical attention was a faithless act that could only be attributed to satanic influence. Even if a loved one was deathly ill no doctor was necessary. Only *faith* that God could heal was the necessary antidote. Again, if someone died it was his/her lack of faith that caused his/her death not the lack of medical attention.[42] And so this became the spiritual atmosphere of our congregation.[43]

---

[42] I remember a man in his early forties that attended our church who believed vehemently that God was going to heal his diabetes. He stopped taking his medication (insulin) and as a result he died due to complications with his blood sugar.

[43] At this point I'd like to tell the story of someone dear to us who fell prey to the fideistic, prophetic hype of the Word-Faith movement at the church we attended, which ultimately left this person and her faith debilitated. (To protect her and her family's privacy I will call her Helen.) One Sunday morning, Helen was prophesied over by an itinerant minister, who told her she was pregnant. Helen's husband was incredulous over the prophetic claim since he was incapable of impregnating his wife on account of having had a vasectomy. For the oracle to be true there could be only three possible explanations: (1) the vasectomy didn't take; (2) Helen was impregnated by another man; or (3) the Holy Spirit impregnated her (as He did Mary, the Mother of our Lord and Savior). There were no reasons to believe (1) and (2), so (3) was the most logical answer from the Word-Faith perspective. After Helen was prophesied over she began to dress in maternity clothes believing that she truly was with child. But after a few months there was no developmental change to her physical stature as one would expect of a pregnant mother. Unfortunately, seeing an obstetrician to check on the development of the baby was out of the question since the faithless act of seeking medical attention was against the by-laws of the church. Helen was encouraged by her spiritual "brothers" and "sisters" not to doubt the prophecy, given all sensible evidence to the contrary since that was tantamount to believing a lie from the pit of hell, rather than believing an oracle from God. So Helen and her husband continued to white-knuckle their faith (i.e., the belief that the baby inside her was immaculately conceived and growing, although they saw no change to her body). This was a definite source of embarrassment and humiliation for the entire family, the children included since they were constantly faced with the devilish possibility that if Helen were not with child it would

I attended a weekly men's prayer meeting where all the men except for me received visions and prophetic words. I believed God was going to give me a word of encouragement for someone, but—for whatever reason—it never happened. I began to believe that maybe there was something wrong with me. So I prayed more fervently for my spiritual gifts to manifest. But again, nothing happened.

After each prayer meeting the men invited me out to dinner. I noticed a pattern emerging: the men would gossip and criticize every person that walked by. This was a great stumbling block for me. I didn't know much theology at the time, but I did know that God is a God of love. So every time they criticized someone, I couldn't get the thought out of my head that their actions were not motivated by love.

Why the presumed accusations? Why the hypocrisy? And why wasn't I receiving prophetic words? The joy I had when I first believed became tainted with confusion and frustration. Eventually, what caused us to leave the church was that one of the well-respected couples there, who were blatantly against modern and natural medicine, ended up going to the hospital to deliver their baby. That was the last straw! I couldn't take the hypocrisy any longer. So I took my family to another church where they believed that God works both in the supernatural and the natural, in the metaphysical and the physical, in the sacred and the secular.

---

be because of their lack of faith. Things only got worse when nine months came and went. Her sisters in the faith abandoned her once the hope of birthing a miracle baby was lost. Vicious rumors spread throughout the church that Helen was not a pious woman. When her own spiritual family turned against her, Helen fell into a deep and debilitating depression. Sadly, Helen fell ill and died a couple of years later.

Chapter 7: Hoops and Hurdles to Get My Commercial Pilot's License

DURING THE SUMMER MONTHS OF CROP-DUSTING, our family experienced a myriad of adventures as we traversed different states. Before our adventures could begin, however, I jumped through many hoops to get my commercial pilot's license with the Federal Aviation Administration (FAA).

After the week I arrived to my brother's home in Gretna, I went to the FAA in New Orleans to find out how I could get a commercial pilot's license. One requirement was to have 300 hours of flight time. I *had* 11,000 flight hours! Another requirement was that I pass both the written and flight test with the FAA.

Eight hours a day for three months, I studied to pass the written test with no avail. My difficulty mastering the English language was the problem. But I continued with my rigorous study habits for another six weeks. Finally, I passed! When I received the good news, I did several somersaults in the living room, much to the delight of my children. That night we all celebrated. Chimba and Rosa Lila came over to José's house where my brother treated everyone to Chinese food.

The next hoop to jump through: the flight test. Happily, I passed with honors due to my extensive flight experience. A couple of weeks later I received a certificate of completion from the FAA that allowed me to fly commercially in any state in the United States. However, getting work flying commercially was another matter.

As it turned out, I could not find work because veteran pilots already took commercial jobs. (I could've worked with the instrument rating experience I had, but that would've limited my flying to only smaller planes that didn't pay enough money considering the risk I was taking.) So I decided to try crop-dusting.

Chapter 8: Kissing Rocks, Bushes and Debris

I TOOK A JOB CROP-DUSTING POTATOES[44] in Munday, Texas. I was called within a week of placing my name on a list of available pilots all over the United States in the widely read aviatic magazine, *Trade-A-Plane*. Sadly, I had to leave my family behind for the sole reason that we couldn't afford lodging for three extra people. It was the summer of 1980.

The days were hot, long, and lonely. Routinely, I would wake up at 4 a.m. to watch the process of poison being poured into the hopper. For my own safety, I wanted to make sure not to take off with more poison than needed. I had to gauge for myself the amount of poison needed given the weather conditions. The reason being is that if the humidity were high I would need less "payload." Considering the fact that I was in Texas during the month of August, it behooved me not to overload the hopper.[45] Routinely, I worked until 8 p.m. everyday, 7 days-a-week, for about 12 weeks, from June to August. As I liked to say, "Insects don't take the weekends off, so neither do I."

Early one evening as dusk started to creep across the horizon, the engine on my Piper PA-25 Pawnee suddenly stopped working. Knowing this meant I had mere minutes to locate the runway for a crash landing, my eyes desperately searched the ground below. Without a lit runway to guide me in, I used my knowledge of the area to determine where to guide the plane. My white knuckles gripped the tiller as I started my descent. I took in a quick inhalation of air as my plane touched down just outside of the landing strip. The belly of the plane kissed rocks, bushes, and debris before jostling onto the runway. After what seemed like an interminably long time, the plane slowed to a stop. Beads of sweat rolled down my face as I safely exited the plane. Expecting to be bawled out by my boss, I was relieved when he slapped me on the back and explained it a "Job well done!" Apparently, he was as surprised as I that such a small plane survived an impromptu landing.

Later, we discovered that the magneto engine ignition system had failed during the flight. I called it "quits" for the summer, never to return to fly in Texas again. (There were rumors circulating that some owners of agricultural bi-planes purposefully tamper with the aircraft to collect the insurance money once the plane crashes.) I booked a flight home the next day on a commercial airline to see the warm, welcoming faces of my family.

The next city the Lord took me to was Corning, Arkansas. Its population of 3,000 people was six times larger than Munday's. This time, I took my family.

---

[44] The veteran crop-dusting pilots sprayed cotton because it was more lucrative. Cotton must be fumigated at least 11-15 times, while potatoes only needed to be sprayed 5-6 times.

[45] These types of crop-dusting planes were dangerous simply because of the layout of the engine (propeller), gas tank, and hopper (poison tank) in relation to the position of the pilot. The pilot sat directly behind the hopper. If the plane came down nose first, then an explosion was almost certain, which meant an imminent death sentence by scorching flames due to a chemical chain reaction of heat, oxygen, poison, and gasoline. The Grumman Ag Cat was the preferred plane that carried fuel in its wings.

The Piper PA-25 Pawnee was an agricultural aircraft produced by Piper for spraying and dusting between 1959 and 1981. I flew this single engine piston plane in Munday, Texas. Summer 1980.

Chapter 9: Crop-Dusting in Arkansas

THE SUMMER OF '81, my wife, two sons and I stayed in a house my boss rented. My morning routine consisted of waking up at 4 a.m. in order to be at work an hour later so I could crop-dust rice and potatoes as soon as the day permitted.[46] But I was also given the duty of planting rice crops via aviation.

This is how it worked: On the ground, I supervised as workers placed a pre-calculated rice load into the hopper. That's right, I said, "hopper." But this time the hopper was cleaned out of poison thoroughly to prevent the rice from sticking to the inside of it. The amount of rice needed was indicative of the crop acreage. Once the rice was loaded I was ready to fly. But this time I was assigned to pilot the superior agricultural aircraft—Grumman G-164 Ag Cat.

Once I was airborne, I would go through my routine checklist: locate the coordinated area with an aeronautical chart; do a once-over flying low to the ground around the field in order to mark any unusual obstructions; and check for wind direction and resistance. Once my checklist was complete, I began to drop my payload.

A usual day consisted of flying from dawn to dusk, anywhere between 5-6 a.m. to 5-6 p.m. When I got home, I was exhausted. But my devoted wife, Myriam, always had a *riquisima* dinner waiting for me; something I looked forward to all throughout the day. Some of my favorites: *arroz aguado con pollo* (boiled rice, chicken, carrots, and potatoes) and *baho* (steamed yuka, tomatoes, green peppers, onions, garlic, ripe and unripe plantains, and beef brisket wrapped in banana leaves).

---

[46] As a craft crop-duster, it's important to start fumigating at the break of dawn before the build up of atmospheric pressure or wind due to the Sun's heat.

JP standing on the left wing of my Grumman G-164 Ag Cat as Myriam and Chestercito sit in the cockpit. Corning, Arkansas. July 1981.

Chapter 10: A Hare Krishna Temple and A Flight to Venezuela

WHEN I FINISHED MY WORK IN CORNING, we left Arkansas to return to Louisiana. In the beginning of '81, we started renting the bottom floor of a two-story duplex at 2942 De Soto Street, New Orleans, from my brother-in-law, Eddie Blais. During this time, I received the joyous news that we had become permanent American residents.

Our duplex, on the corner of De Soto Street and Gayoso Avenue, was directly across from a Hare Krishna temple. This area of New Orleans was a gumbo of cultures, languages and religions. Simply stepping out my front door bombarded me with unfamiliar cooking smells wafting down alleyways; foreign words tumbling down porch steps; and American street fashion flashing by on sidewalks. One thing did feel very familiar, however: the sticky, sweaty feel of my shirt stuck to my skin during the humid summer months, just like it once did in Managua.

Five days a week—from midnight to 8 a.m.—I worked as a security guard at the New Orleans Marriott on Canal Street. Management liked the fact that I had a military background, and I soon discovered why: the number of suspicious and threatening characters who would haunt the streets at those hours required someone with a steely nerve and rigid training to maintain a professional, yet ever-vigilant watch.

While we were living in New Orleans, my half-brother—David Delagneau—came to visit us from Venezuela. (He was my half-brother from my father's side.) I told him about my struggle to find equal work and thus pay in the States compared to Nicaragua. He then told me about the vast opportunities to fumigate all types of crop in Venezuela. He made it sound like everything was set up for me there to make as much money as I'd made crop-dusting in Nicaragua, which was up to $60,000 per season, during the summer months.

With great optimism, I immediately booked a flight to Venezuela. But upon my arrival, I quickly discovered that getting a job would be much more difficult than either one of us had anticipated. Even if I were to get my pilot's license there, I'd only get the jobs the locals didn't want, which meant I'd make—at most—half of what I'd made in Nicaragua. So I decided it wasn't lucrative to stay and take my chances there. After all, I was already working in New Orleans, and I'd be closer to my family.

Myriam standing outside the front of our De Soto house across the street from the Hare Krishna Temple after church on Sunday. In the background, one can see the taillight of a green '74 Chevy Vega. Chimba gave the car to us as a gift. Spring 1981.

Chestercito (8) and JP (4¾) playing by the Bayou St. John, New Orleans. Spring 1981.

Chestercito (7½) and JP (4) got into Myriam's makeup. The boys are proudly modeling their painted faces on our tweed, plaid couch in our De Soto home. Summer 1981.

Saying goodbye to Chester at the Louis Armstrong
New Orleans International Airport. He was leaving
to Venezuela to get his pilot's license to work there
for the season. Summer 1981.

Chestercito (8) and JP (4½) playing in front of our De Soto home. Fall 1981.

Chestercito (8) and JP (4½) hanging on Chester at our De Soto home. Notice the vintage television, yellow pinewood door and green shag carpet in the background. Winter 1981.

Our first Christmas at our De Soto home. JP (4½) hugging his blowup Santa Claus on Christmas Day. 1981.

Chapter 11: "Old Faithful"

Bison herd grazing as Old Faithful geyser erupts. Photo courtesy of www.pixabay.com.

IT WASN'T UNTIL JUNE 11, 1982 that I was contacted about another crop-dusting job through *Trade-A-Plane*. This time, it would take me to Rexburg, Idaho. I informed the Marriot that I needed to take an extended leave of absence in order to crop-dust for the summer. On June 14, I boarded a commercial airline, once again having to say goodbye to my family.

Upon arrival, my boss alerted me to the fact that the potato crop had frozen over and thus my work would be delayed. I remember impatiently waiting daily for the warmth of the sun to defrost the 2,000-acre crop. A week went by with no work. I ached to go home, but my boss had it in good authority from the Idaho State Department of Agriculture that I could start work within a week.

When it was time, I jumped into my Ag Cat in order to fertilize the potato crop before commencing fumigation. On the days I was prevented from working due to inclement weather, Ray—my boss for 2 ½ months—took me across the border to Wyoming to fish and enjoy the beautiful spectacle of "Old Faithful" at Yellowstone National Park. I remember him telling me that the cone geyser erupts on the hour shooting approximately 4,000 gallons of boiling water toward the heavens to an average height of 145 feet.

Celebrating Damarita's 18th birthday at José's house. Left to right: Myriam, Damaris, Lixio, José and Damarita. Gretna. April 9, 1982.

Dance party at our De Soto home. Summer 1982.

Chapter 12: Mardi Gras at the Marriott (Rated-R)

I RETURNED HOME TO RESUME MY WORK AS A SECURITY GUARD at the Marriott when my work was done in Idaho. My responsibilities were to keep the hotel lobby free of wanton workers and to secure the two towers that reached 36 floors each from burglars. This was no easy feat given that it took about two hours to walk up each tower, which included patrolling the hallways of each floor.

Bourbon Street in the French Quarter—known for its bars and strip clubs—was only three streets away from the hotel. This made my job challenging given the year round influx of drunkards, prostitutes, and homeless people looking to continue having a good time in the hallways, elevators, restrooms, and stairwells. But by far the most stressful time of year at the Marriott was during Mardi Gras, also known as "Fat Tuesday."

Fat Tuesday initially represented the practice of eating richer, fatty foods before Ash Wednesday, which commenced the ritual fasting of Lenten season. But for younger, more promiscuous Mardi Grasers, it's simply an excuse to be drunken exhibitionists. Every year, from February to March, people come to the French Quarter from all around the world to celebrate this carnival season for a raucous and debaucherous good time.

Mardi Gras, New Orleans. Photo by skeeze courtesy of www.pixabay.com.

It was during Mardi Gras of '83 that I encountered a horrific incident at the Marriott. We were all on high security alert. I was assigned to work "base" so I was constantly being informed of the wild parties in both towers. Suddenly, I received a distress call from a guest in one of the rooms. Loud screams penetrated from next door. I immediately called 911 and dispatched all security guards to the room in question.

We soon learned that a black male stabbed a white woman in front of her husband with a broken alcohol container. Security arrived three minutes later to apprehend the perpetrator. Shortly thereafter, the local police showed up to interrogate the perp. The report of both the black man and the husband matched up: In a Bourbon Street bar, the couple propositioned a black man to have sex with both of them in their Marriott hotel room. But the proposition did not go as planned: after the black man had intercourse with the wife, he refused to have sex with the husband and that's when things got heated. The husband refused to pay him, so the man broke a glass bottle and stabbed the woman down in her private parts. And that's when the neighbors heard her scream. Afterwards, the management at the hotel implemented a stricter guest code of conduct to minimize the chance a night like that would ever happen again.

Four months later, I was contacted through *Trade-A-Plane* by Mr. Henderson to fumigate his sugar cane crop.

Chapter 13: Sugar Cane Fields

MY NEW JOB TOOK ME TO HOUMA, Louisiana. My family would come down from New Orleans to stay the weekends in a motorhome that my boss rented. At the time, Myriam was working as a manager of a small Spanish restaurant called *Camacho* on Saint Charles Avenue, an affluent area in New Orleans, so only weekend visits were possible. Unfortunately, there was not much for my family to do while I was working. Nevertheless, Chestercito and JP loved playing in the trailer park. When they weren't running around, Myriam would take them to a nearby swamp where they would throw rocks and watch them disappear into the murky waters.

For me, fumigating sugar cane fields made things easier in some ways. Crop-dusting potatoes typically involved fumigating a crop 5-6 times in a season as I flew 2-4 feet above the potato fields. But with sugar cane fields, I only needed to fumigate the same crop 4-5 times in a season, and I could fly 8 feet above the fields, mitigating my chances of crashing or hitting debris from being so close to the ground. That summer, however, I ran into a problem.

My boss assigned a new hire to pump gas into my Ag Cat. Once the plane was full, I took off to spray the crops. That's when I noticed something was wrong with the plane: the temperature gauge was running hot and the pressure gauge was low. Also, I noticed that the exhaust was a bit darker than usual. But I didn't want to double-back just yet. I was afraid of possibly ruining the landing gear since the poison's full weight puts more pressure on the belly of the plane during landing. So, once I finished my payload, I returned to base.

A mechanic checked the plane and discovered that diesel fuel was the culprit. The "green" hire unknowingly put diesel fuel that was used for tractors into the aircraft. This undoubtedly ruined the engine and since my boss owned only one plane, this ended my season. Once I got paid, I left for home and started working again at the Marriott.

Earlier that year, Myriam started John Jay Beauty School full-time, working diligently to graduate in the fall. She passed her state exam—Louisiana State Board of Cosmetology—on October 14, 1983. Who would've known that Myriam would still be styling hair until this day, although now it's for the elderly at our board-and-care homes? To everyone who sits in her chair, she is a beacon of light. She listens with a compassionate ear to every word her clients say and she reflects the love of the Father by offering to pray for them.

Myriam starting John Jay Beauty School. New Orleans. January 1983.

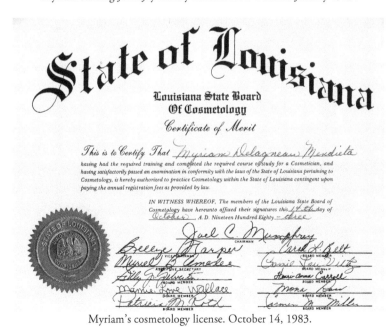

Myriam's cosmetology license. October 14, 1983.

Sunday after church upstairs in Martin's house on De Soto St. JP (6) sitting with Mildred, Lucho and their dog, Dolly. New Orleans. Fall 1983.

Our last Christmas at our De Soto home. 1983.

Chapter 14: Sizzling Cajun Barbeque Chicken

THERE WAS NEVER A DULL MOMENT LIVING ON DE SOTO STREET. Our neighbor to the left was a private Italian woman, who, strangely enough, let a day laborer—my sons called "Spider-Man"—live with her in a small bedroom downstairs. Across the way to the right, lived four gay men, who enjoyed throwing flamboyant parties on the weekends. Next to them lived a Caucasian family. The youngest daughter, Jennifer, was Chestercito's good friend that he liked to call "Ghee." To the right of them lived another white family. Their youngest son, Paul, was also Jr.'s close friend. Directly across the street from us was a two-story home that was renovated into a Hare Krishna temple. The Hare Krishnas were friendly, hospitable people willing to share with anyone their religious beliefs and food offered to Krishna, who's considered a major Hindu god and the eighth incarnation of Vishnu. Bayou Saint John, which feeds off Lake Pontchartrain, was located four blocks west. One block east of the bayou was Holy Rosary School, which the boys attended for several years. Three blocks northwest of us was our favorite eatery, Liuzza's, known for its affordable, delicious food. The boys enjoyed their anchovy pizza, onion rings, and frosty mugs of soda. The quickest route to Liuzza's was Esplanade Avenue. Less than a mile west on Esplanade from Liuzza's was City Park, a local favorite family hangout. On several occasions we arranged to have all our extended families gather together at City Park. As usual, Chimba manned the grill. I can still remember the sound and taste of his sizzling Cajun barbeque chicken.

Chestercito with "Uncle Eddie" barbequing his specialty—Cajun chicken
and yams on his portable charcoal grill at City Park located one block
south of Lake Pontchartrain. We were still living with José and his family.
New Orleans. Summer 1980.

At City Park with Eddie's family. Left to right: Myriam, Chestercito, me and my sister, Rosa Lila. New Orleans. Summer 1980.

Chestercito's 9th birthday party with JP to the far right and their friend, Paul, in the middle at our De Soto home. It must've been afterschool on a weekday because Chestercito is still wearing his Holy Rosary School t-shirt. New Orleans. October 15, 1982.

Myriam and Chestercito with his prized stuffed animal leaving Pontchartrain Beach Amusement Park. Winter 1983.

Chapter 15: Gushing Blood and An Attempted Carjacking

THERE ARE TWO UNFORGETTABLE STORIES THAT HAPPENED TO ME—Myriam—while we were living on De Soto Street that should not be forgotten. The first is the story of a pastor friend who was assaulted, and the second involved an attempted carjacking.

It was the summer of '81. The boys were little: Chestercito was seven years old and JP was four. We were planning on leaving early the next morning to be with my husband who was crop-dusting in Arkansas. In the evening, I arranged a prayer meeting with a young pastor from Honduras named Cirilo, asking for God's blessings in the form of provisions and protection on our trip. We worshipped the Lord until about 10 p.m. I walked him to the door and said goodnight. Moments later, I heard screaming and banging on the door.

Fear gripped my heart. I could hear his voice from the other side of the door screaming my name. I rushed to open it and witnessed blood gushing from his hand. I ran to the kitchen to retrieve coffee grounds, which helps coagulate blood, and I bandaged his finger with Columbian caffeine. As I wrapped, the story tumbled from his white lips: On his way to his car, two black men emerged from the shadows and assaulted him. In their struggle to steal his graduation ring, they nearly tore off his finger to get it. Once they ran off, he made his way back to our house for aid.

One might think that what happened was ironic: we had just prayed for protection and then a short while later, he got attacked. But I view it as an example of spiritual warfare. By praying for us, he supernaturally invoked God's blessing on us, shifting the spiritual atmosphere in our favor. Seeing his act of faith, no doubt angered the demonic powers that be, inciting retaliation—be it spiritual or physical.

My second story happened that summer. One evening, I was watching the local news report about a criminal ruse to steal automobiles. Their technique was subtle: they 'accidentally' collided with the vehicle in front of them so the driver would emerge from the car to exchange information. Once the driver exited the car, a person hiding in the rear car would sneak into the driver's seat of the victim's vehicle. His partner in crime would run back to his automobile and they would both take off—sometimes killing the victim if needed.

The following evening, I was driving alone down the hot, humid streets, looking forward to seeing my family and resting my tired body. Just as I pulled onto our street, I heard a metallic crunch behind me. My body instantly tensed as the memory of the news report flooded my brain. Reacting quickly, I locked the doors as my car idled in the middle of the street directly in front of our house. Behind me, the driver got out and walked up to where I was sitting. I immediately laid on the horn. Panicked, the man ran back to his car and sped off without his headlights on, preventing me from identifying the vehicle's license plate number. Shaking, I drove our dented car into the driveway and ran into the house.

I consider this sinister situation another opportunity to boast about God's protection over my life. Sure, our only car was damaged (the one Chimba had so generously donated to us), requiring repair and spending money we didn't have. But I felt blessed to be alive and know God's hand of protection was over my family and me. Christ tells us, "In this world you will have trouble. But take heart! I have overcome the world" (John 16:33b, NIV).

Chapter 16: Cowboy

IN THE FALL OF '83, Myriam and I talked it over and we decided I should go to California and personally hand-in some applications to crop-dust cotton fields. They were the most profitable of all the fumigation crops. We prayed and then I left right away. I called my cousin-in-law—Alex Pinell—who lived in Huntington Beach to expect my arrival and asked that he drive me to San Joaquin Valley, also known as the Promised Land of crop-dusting in California. I turned in about 30 applications on that trip.

On my way home, Alex and his wife, Yolanda (my first cousin), accompanied me to Las Vegas for a few days. We stayed at a kitsch hotel-casino called Circus Circus. When I got back home, I resubmitted my flight information to *Trade-A-Plane*.

During my trip to "The Golden State," I immediately became enamored with the moderately cool climate, clean neighborhoods, award-winning schools and the energizing feel of economic prosperity. When I got back home, I told Myriam, "We're moving! Alex and Yolanda offered to have us stay with them until we can find a place of our own."

Three months later, on New Year's Day—1984—with butterflies in our stomachs and thoughts of golden sunsets over the Pacific Ocean, we commenced our cross-country trek. We rented a U-Haul trailer and packed my sky blue '79 Chevrolet Impala to the gills. I remember that morning was especially chilly, but thoughts of our new home in sunny California energized us for the trek west.

It took us exactly five days to make the trip, one more day than anticipated to fix a fuel problem. On average, I drove 12 hours per day. We covered about 550 miles the first day arriving in San Antonio, Texas, that evening. Hungry and tired, we went to dinner and found a motel to spend the night. We were on the road the next morning at 9 a.m. after breakfast and showers.

Every day held new challenges and adventures. For example, just as we tacked on another 600 miles to the car, driving through New Mexico, the engine caught on fire. I remember that it was dark and rainy that evening. The kids were asleep in the back. I immediately pulled the car over and yelled, "Fire! Fire! Get out!" The family spilled out of the car. But now I was worried that the car was no longer drivable. "How am I going to pay to get a new engine?" "How long's that going to take?" A local mechanic, who'd witnessed what had happened, came over and helped me extinguish the fire. He recommended I leave the car at his garage so he could take care of it in the morning. I acquiesced, hardly sleeping a wink that night, worried that we might be robbed or held up at gunpoint.

The town we stayed in—somewhere between Las Cruces and Deming—was small, so small in fact that there was only one mechanic shop, one motel, one road (I-10), and no restaurants, no fire station or police station. We were at the mercy of this dilapidated ole place. As soon as the sun came up, I arrived at the garage anxious to find out the damage and cost to my vehicle.

As it turned out, the fire was the result of a gas leak in the fuel hose. Like I said, I was at the mercy of whatever the town had to offer: the mechanic could have charged me an arm-and-a-leg but he didn't. I think I paid around $60 for both the new hose and the labor. We left that blessing-of-a-town about noon and headed to our next destination: Phoenix, Arizona. That day we drove about half our normal distance (around 350 miles). We had a terrible night's sleep the day before, so we were looking forward to staying in a nice hotel. We ate a delicious dinner, slept in till 8 a.m., gorged ourselves on bacon and eggs for breakfast, and then left about 9 a.m. for San Diego, arriving there at 4 p.m. (about 350 miles later).

I remember calling Alex from a gas station payphone to let him know where we were. Excitedly, he instructed us to wait for him so he could personally escort us back to his home in Huntington Beach. While awaiting his arrival, we ate an early dinner at Burger King; about an hour later, we all met. *Besitos y abrazos* were exchanged.

After a warm welcome, we caravanned the final stretch of our trip (the last 100 miles). On January 5, 1984 we arrived at our new home—7552 Volga Drive.

In front of the Cowboy after lunch with Alex and Yolanda. Las Vegas. 1983.

PART III
California

Chapter 1: The Lord Smiled Down on Us

Myriam and I sitting on the floor of Alex's house. Huntington Beach. January 1984.

WE STAYED WITH YOLANDA, ALEX AND ALEX, JR., in their apartment for several months until we could find an apartment of our own. As we looked for a place nearby, so the boys could remain in the school a block away at Sun View Elementary, Myriam and I tirelessly studied to pass our state examinations as beautician and pilot. Just before we moved out, we pulled the trigger, taking our respective exams and staying true to our professions. As we awaited our test results, we walked the neighborhood and knocked on doors to retrieve any information about the renter and/or the monthly rental fee.

At this point, a problem became blatantly apparent to us: every renter we talked to denied our rental application on the spot due to the fact that we were jobless, and it didn't help matters much that we were immigrants. We also hadn't yet received word about our license status; we were quickly becoming desperate.

Then the Lord smiled down on us in the form of an older married Italian lady, named Anna Pappas Hips. She took one look at my application and then one look at me and said, "The locals rent from me and they don't pay me. But foreigners pay on time. The place is yours." We moved in the next day.

At church celebrating our first Easter in California. Fountain Valley. April 1984.

Chapter 2: Establish a Clientele

NOT LONG AFTER, we received a letter in the mail saying that I—Myriam—passed my cosmetology license exam. I was now Board of Barbering and Cosmetology certified in California. I started working right away at Hana's Hair Salon in Huntington Beach.

At first, due to my inexperience, the owner said I could earn only 60% commission. This, of course, was not ideal. So Chester and I prayed about the best way to establish a clientele. We made flyers and passing them out within a two-mile radius of the salon. Within two months, my clientele grew expeditiously and I arranged, in lieu of paying commission, to only pay rent for the occupied space. I rented my own booth from Hana for one year.

During that time, I remember going out of my way to pick up some of my clients from their home so I could style their hair at the salon. A mother, aged 90, and her daughter, aged 75, were no longer driving. So I agreed to not only be their hairdresser but also their chauffeur. They were a quirky, funny couple. The mother's favorite joke she told everyone each time she entered the salon was: "What is the Mexican weather? Chili today. Hot tamale."

Chapter 3: Back to Studying

ABOUT A WEEK LATER, I—Chester—received a letter in the mail from the California Agricultural Aircraft Association (CAAA), but with a different result. Unfortunately, I had failed the written exam. Back to studying I went. Two weeks later I took it again. This time I passed. I wasted no time applying in person for a crop-dusting job in San Joaquin Valley.

In the span of a weekend, I must've shaken at least ten different owners' hands. Five days later, I received a phone call from Fresno asking me to come up for the day to fill in for a sick pilot. I told them that I didn't feel comfortable coming up for such a short period of time because I would need more time to acquire information on the lay of the land, including low hanging power lines, crop routes and boundaries, as well as weather conditions. They were not happy with my response, which is probably why I never heard from them again. I did, however, hear from an aviation company in North Dakota, thanks to *Trade-A-Plane* magazine. They wanted me to fly for the season and start in a week. I agreed, flying out the next day.

I have pleasant memories of fumigating grains in the small town of Rugby, North Dakota, a population of what seemed like 300 people. My boss (I think his name was John) was a good man, who cared about the needs of his pilots and clients. I remember him being tall and strong, the quintessential American mid-western man, reared on a steady diet of meat and potatoes. Next to me, he looked like a giant. I, on the other hand, could barely keep any meat on my bones with my detritus diet of frozen dinners for breakfast, lunch and dinner.

Rugbians were made up largely of Caucasians with a small percentage of Indians. The climate was delightful in summer months, not too hot and not too cold—the Goldilocks of weather. The landscape, however, was not much to write home about from the ground: low-hanging power lines, windmills that power farms, and green plains as far as the eye can see. But from the cockpit flying at 200 feet, crop fields looked like offset squares of jungle adjacent to lush prairies. Unfortunately, when my job was done in August of '84, I never returned to fumigate in North Dakota, again. I called home to tell my wife that I'd be seeing her real soon. I left the next day.

Chapter 4: Thrive Not Just Survive

WHEN I GOT HOME I FOUND MYSELF JOBLESS. In Louisiana, I was used to working for a large hotel company as a security guard between crop-dusting seasons. But here in California, I didn't know what to do. But that all changed when my cousin, Nicasio Garcia, came to visit me from his home nearby. We talked about life and family. Eventually, we got around to talking about our vocations. I told him I was currently unemployed, but Myriam was making good money as a beautician. If it weren't for her income we would not have been able to pay for necessities, such as food, rent, clothes, and gas. We were barely getting by. But I wanted our family to thrive not just survive.

Nicasio encouraged me to go with him to a car auction in Norwalk. As it turned out, my cousin made a living buying and selling used cars. I watched him go from car to car looking meticulously under hoods and listening attentively to engines for clean headers and cylinders. He wasn't a mechanic, but he made working with cars look easy. So I thought, why not me? The following Tuesday, I went back with Nicasio and I bought two cars—one Honda and one Toyota. They only needed a wash. In a week, I was able to sell both. Every week after that, I returned to buy one or two cars. With the money I made, I put 80% into savings and with the leftover 20%, I invested it back into my new car business.

Chapter 5: Renewing Our Wedding Vows

MYRIAM AND I DECIDED TO RENEW OUR WEDDING VOWS on her 34th birthday, March 13, 1985. This made it our 11-year wedding anniversary. We were living in our own apartment on 7551 Amazon Drive in Huntington Beach. With Myriam working full-time as a beautician and me working two jobs—one as a used car salesman and the other as a crop-dusting pilot—we needed to slow down our lives and enjoy each other. So we made it a priority to meet with our pastor at lunchtime one day to have him marry us. I asked Myriam all over again if she would be my faithfully wedded wife. She said, "I do." Then she asked me if I would love her all the days of her life. And I said, "I do."

On our knees professing our love to one another all over again. Fountain Valley. March 13, 1985.

With our pastor after the wedding ceremony. For this special occasion we went to the Los Angeles Garment District to purchase my dress and Chester's suit. Fountain Valley. March 13, 1985.

Celebrating my 34th birthday at our Amazon home on the same day Chester and I renewed our wedding vows. From left to right: Damaris, me, Orlanda (Damaris's friend and my client at the hair salon) and Chestercito. Huntington Beach. March 13, 1985.

Chapter 6: Highly Recommended

PRIOR TO HARVEST SEASON THE FOLLOWING YEAR, I received an interesting phone call. The manager of a small crop-dusting company in Hot Springs, South Dakota, said that I came highly recommended by another pilot, whom I only met once when I was flying up north. I agreed to start work in June of '85 but because of inclement weather conditions in Hot Springs, I didn't book a flight until the beginning of July. Once I arrived in the small town of about 300-400 people, the manager was waiting for me in his pick-up truck with some bad news.

Because of the weeklong rainstorm, the majority of the crops had drowned. I waited there a few days hoping that the situation would change so I would not have to go back home empty-handed. I called Myriam every day looking forward to the sound of her voice and hoping to talk to my boys. I needed something positive to distract me from what was happening 1,200 miles away from home. And as God would have it, the remaining crops started to grow. That meant that I could start fumigating right away, which I eagerly did.

Flying an Ag Cat similar to the one in North Dakota, I fumigated grains like I did up north. The main difference in dusting is that the fields in Rugby are square-shaped, unlike the irregular ones in Hot Springs. As any crop-duster can tell you, circular or triangular-shaped fields are a waste of time and money. Also, I was only in South Dakota half the time I was up north, which meant half the money. I left as soon as the season was over in August.

The neighborhood boys at the beach south of the Huntington Beach pier. Left to right: Noel, Albert, JP and Chestercito. August 1985.

Chapter 7: Pulkrabek

BETWEEN CROP-DUSTING SEASONS, I continued to sell used cars that I purchased from car auctions in Norwalk, Anaheim, and Los Angeles. At this point, I started getting into my groove when it came to buying and selling cars. I was up to six cars, but encountered problems with storage. My neighbors were getting upset with me because I was taking up space parking the cars on the street. I constantly kept moving my vehicles in order to keep the neighbors happy. Meanwhile, the next crop season was looming. So I put in another ad into *Trade-A-Plane*. The year was 1986. It would be my last season flying, and for good reason.

I received a phone call in late May from Tom Pulkrabek, the owner of a small crop-dusting company with four airplanes, called Pulkrabek, in Minnesota. He wanted me to be on the next plane to Fargo. I arrived June 1st, which I think was a weekday. He picked me up and took me to a restaurant to talk about the ins-and-outs of the company, the expectations of the customers, and the vital responsibilities that I'd be yoked to for the next three months. I was made well-aware that I had to take good care of my aircraft, another Ag Cat, because it would be the only plane I would be flying for the duration of the season.

After dinner, he took me to his hanger in the small town of Angus, about an hour-and-a-half from Fargo. He showed me my sleeping quarters, located in his office, measuring only 144 square feet. As soon as he left, I made one phone call to Myriam, and then fell onto my camp-bed-folding-cot like a lightning bolt during a lightning storm. For the next seven hours I was dead to the world.

I awoke the next morning at 4 a.m. and quickly shaved and showered. Then, I did my homework that consisted mainly of familiarizing myself with my flight plan. Flying from dusk to dawn, I fumigated grains. Robotically, I followed this work regimen for the next few days until the rain prevented me from flying.

Tom invited me to his house that weekend to meet his family. His wife cooked us a delicious meal as we swapped stories about our lives and time spent flying.

Red jumpsuit. Angus, Minnesota.
August 1986.

Standing on top of Pulkrabek's plane after dusting. A fuel error made me return to base prematurely. In this picture,
I'm not wearing my jumpsuit on account of it being washed. Because of constant exposure to agricultural poison and gas fumes,
my clothes needed to be washed daily. Angus, Minnesota. August 1986.

Chapter 8: "It Was the Best of Times, It Was the Worst of Times"

A COUPLE OF WEEKS AFTER I STARTED FLYING, two veteran crop-dusting pilots in their 60s arrived. They, like I, worked tirelessly day in and day out to get the job done. It was when our crop-dusting season was nearly over that tragedy struck.

The day started like any other: early morning flights to fumigate with stops back at the hangar to reload the hopper. By mid-afternoon, I was once again reloading my plane when an airplane attendant ran over with the devastating news of a crash.

According to the attendant, Pilot 1 had just finished dropping his payload of poison and was in motion of turning his aircraft to re-engage the crops at about 50 feet above the earth. Pilot 2 took off and left the runway low to the ground never ascending passed 50 feet. He was headed to fumigate his own field when, unexpectedly, the top of his plane hit the belly of the other. Once the attendant finished speaking, I tore off like a light to see for myself, fear sinking its claws into my heart. From bird's-eye-view, I could see a ring of fire surrounding the remains of the planes engulfed in smoke. They looked like two hunks of burnt, twisted metal.

With the pilots' gruesome deaths haunting me, I finished off the season. Every time I was in the air, I couldn't help but think of my friends and their twisted fate, knowing how their poor families must be suffering. I came home that season feeling different. I felt like God was telling me that my career as a pilot had come to an end.

But flying was all I knew. It was my identity—an air force pilot for my home country (Nicaragua) and my new country (United States), as well as a crop-dusting pilot for both. I had been a pilot for 27 years from '59 to '86. I extended my wings wherever the wind took me. But not anymore.

My wings were now being clipped. After a stressful and sad season, I'd finally be able to see my family again, especially my wife, who was now pregnant with our little girl. Now I know what Charles Dickens felt when he penned in *A Tale of Two Cities*: "It was the best of times, it was the worst of times…"

Chapter 9: Set Up, Beaten and Mugged

WHEN I RETURNED HOME, I continued to sell used cars. But now that I was no longer flying, I came up with a new way to make more money for our growing family. Fellow Nicaragüenses, Connie Arguello and Enrique Bermudez—two recent friends of ours—would prove to be instrumental in the next chapter of my career.

Connie was selling jewelry and making double what she paid for it. My friend Enrique shared that he was going door-to-door selling life insurance. He also had a sister-in-law selling jewelry retail; she would go up to Los Angeles regularly to buy it wholesale in order to make a profit. A plan began to formulate in my mind: I figured I, too, could buy jewelry wholesale and then sell it to Enrique's clients at a profit, offering him a small kickback in return. When he agreed to this proposal, I hit the ground running.

Shortly after starting my jewelry business, Myriam and I decided to host jewelry parties with people we knew and trusted. Myriam did her best to help me while being under doctor's orders for partial bed rest. On the weekends, we would host jewelry socials in our friends' homes all around Orange and Los Angeles Counties, including Garden Grove, Huntington Beach, Westminster, Hawaiian Gardens and Norwalk.

It was a great time to be buying and selling jewelry. The fall months typically yielded the best profit margins with Christmas being just around the corner. The year 1986 proved to be an interesting time in the world: The Oprah Winfrey Show debuted nationally and Haley's Comet flashed her tail across the sky.

To more somber news, Chernobyl had exploded and the Iran-Contra Affair became public. Not as dramatic as Irangate, but certainly as important was the news from a friend that I was going to be set up, beaten and mugged in Hawaiian Gardens during a routine pickup of jewelry money (about $3000) that several clients owed me. My line of work was not without risk, and once again, God showed His hand of protection over me.

After I was tipped-off to the impending heist, I never returned to the place of my would-be-demise, although I continued to sell jewelry. Thanks to the money Myriam was making as a beautician and I was making selling jewelry, we enjoyed a wonderful family Christmas in Huntington Beach that year—our last before making the move to Mission Viejo. As we celebrated, we thanked the Lord for the priceless gift of His begotten Son and the precious gift of our first daughter, soon to be born in the New Year.

Costume party at the Arguello's home. Buena Park. October 1985.

Christmas Eve party at the Campos's home. JP (8½) wrapped in presents.
Buena Park. 1985.

Flying to Louisiana. Summer 1986.

Family picture. Left to right: (back) Chimba, Jared, Martin, Rolando holding Maggie, Damarita and Lucho; (front) Leslie, Chestercito, Lixio, Myriam, Mildred, JP, Matthew and Ruby. Algiers. Summer 1986.

Chestercito (almost 13) posing for his individual picture as goalie for his soccer team, The Surfs. Huntington Beach. September 1986.

JP (9¼) posing for his individual picture for his soccer team, The Silver Bullets. Huntington Beach. September 1986.

Chapter 10: "It's a Girl!"

Feeding Crystalina after her 2-week check-up. Huntington Beach. February 1987.

CRYSTAL "CRYSTALINA" ELIZABETH DELAGNEAU was born on January 30, 1987 at 2 p.m. in Fountain Valley Regional Hospital four months before we moved into our new home in Mission Viejo. All my colleagues at John Coiffeur Hair Salon were betting that the baby would be born a healthy baby girl. And she was. She was perfect! Crystal weighed 6 lb, 6 oz. Friends and family carrying cards and balloons (and I believe that a champagne bottle was smuggled in) came to see me at the hospital. Four days later, we got to take our baby home.

Returning to our apartment in Huntington Beach with the baby girl whom I'd been praying for was a dream come true. I remember that we hardly had to buy anything for our daughter. All my friends and clients at the salon threw me a generous baby shower, gifting me with diapers, bottles and blankets. And my family pitched in to buy us a baby carrier and stroller. With two beautiful boys and now a precious little girl, my heart was full to overflowing with God's blessings.

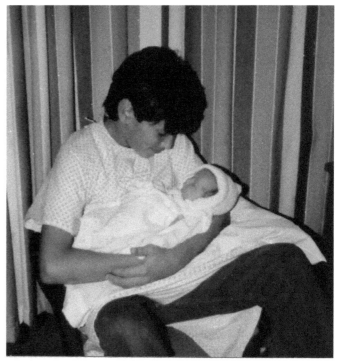

Chestercito (13) holding his baby sister at the Fountain Valley Regional Hospital. February 1, 1987.

Celebrating my 36th birthday a week late. Crystalina is about 2-months-old. Mission Viejo. March 21, 1987.

JP 3rd grade at Sun View Elementary.
Spring 1987.

Chestercito's 7th grade at Park View Junior High.
Spring 1987.

(We moved from Huntington Beach to
Mission Viejo in May. So Jr.'s school friend,
Chris Martin, invited him to stay with him
and his family for the remainder of the school
year. We're extremely thankful for everything
Chris's family did for our son during that time.)

Mother's Day with Crystalina (almost 4-months-old). Mission Viejo. May 10, 1987.

Celebrating JP's 10th birthday with his Huntington Beach friends at our new home in Mission Viejo. Left to right: (back) me holding Crystalina, Tony, Nathan, Damarita, JP, Mercedes and Daniel Collins. June 7, 1987.

Damarita and José Tomás's wedding. Left to right: Victoria Isabel ("Coco"), me, Chestercito, Damarita, José Tomás, (front) JP,
Chester and Ramón Emilio. St. Pius V Catholic Church. Buena Park. January 10, 1987.

Visiting Louisiana. Chester with his brother and mother at Mildred's house. Gretna. 1987.

Chapter 11: Naturalized Citizens

CHESTER AND I STUDIED FOR YEARS TO BECOME NATURALIZED CITIZENS OF THE UNITED STATES OF AMERICA. To receive our certificates of naturalization (or what we like to call "diplomas"), we had to have a basic understanding of U.S. history and government, as well as to read, write and speak basic English.

It meant the world to us to become citizens of a country that took us in when we were violently torn away from our motherland's bosom. Up to this point, we've been blessed as residents to suckle from the breast of a land of milk and honey that values and fights for the freedoms we've lost from our anthropological motherland. Over time, we've begun to thirst and crave the sweet nectar of liberty, at times, however, fearing that it was all a dream. But now that dream has become a reality: now we receive the right to travel to most countries, to vote in national elections and to work anywhere in the U.S. without the fear of being deported back to Nicaragua.

But, oh Nicaragua, Nicaragüita, how we still miss you. We remember the rich memories you provided us that made us who we are—the deep, dark soil from which we were planted. Our roots intertwined to strengthen our support for each other. You let us bear fruit just before we sprouted wings. It's because of your innate goodness and tenderness the poet sings:

> Ay Nicaragua, Nicaragüita,
> La flor mas linda de mi querer,
> Abonada con la bendita,
> Nicaragüita, sangre de Diriangén.
> Ay Nicaragua sos mas dulcita,
> Que la mielita de Tamagas,
> Pero ahora que ya sos libre,
> Nicaragüita, yo te quiero mucho mas.
> Pero ahora que ya sos libre,
> Nicaragüita, yo te quiero mucho mas.
> —Famous Folk Song "Nicaragua, Nicaragüita"
> written by Carlos Mejía Godoy

> Oh Nicaragua, sweet Nicaragua,
> The most beautiful flower I could ever desire,
> Paid with the blessed,
> Blood of [the martyr] Diriangén.
> Oh Nicaragua, you are more sweet,
> Than the honey of the Tamagas [tree favored by honey bees]
> But now that you are free, dear Nicaragua,
> I love you much more.
> But now that you are free, dear Nicaragua,
> I love you much more.
> —Translation of "Nicaragua, Nicaragüita"
> by Chester J. Delagneau, Jr.

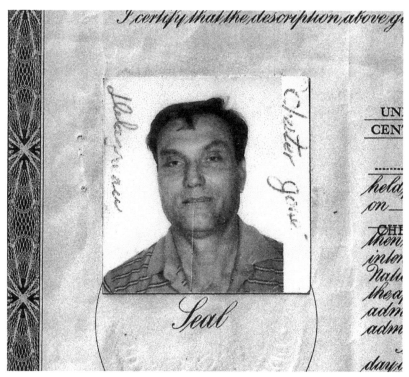

I received my certificate of naturalization on September 23, 1987. This is my picture and signature only. I'm not able to provide a complete copy of my certificate on account of it being "punishable by U.S. law to copy, print or photograph this certificate."

The day I—Chester—received my "diploma" was one of the happiest of my life. I remember being at the Los Angeles Convention Center for the ceremony. It was Friday around noontime. The governor at the time—George Deukmejian—gave a powerful speech rousing the crowd. He talked about how his parents were Armenian immigrants who emigrated from the Ottoman Empire in the 1900s to escape from the Armenian Genocide. He also spoke about how he, himself, started from humble beginnings, working hard to become a lawyer, Long Beach state assemblyman, California state senator, Attorney General of California and eventually becoming the 35th Governor of California. At the end of his speech, he inspired the 500 of us in the arena awaiting citizenship by saying, "If I can make it in this country, any one of you can be whatever you want to be!" Then we were called up to receive our certificates of naturalization. That's when we heard the American national anthem, which we all proceeded to sing.

That evening, we invited our friends and family over to our new home in Mission Viejo to celebrate with us.

I received my certificate of naturalization on October 12, 1988. This is my picture and signature only.

I—Myriam—remember that that day as both solemn and surreal. The day I longed for was finally happening! All of my hard work was about to pay off: hours spent studying American history and government; working daily as part-owner, administrator and caregiver for our new board and care business for the elderly, Glorious Homes; and caring for our three children.

As we were called up to receive our "diplomas," I remember watching Neil Diamond singing "America" on the big screen. Tears flowed down the faces around me as participants spontaneously joined in the singing. I truly was proud to be an American!

We invited our friends and family that evening to join us in celebrating my naturalization as a U.S. citizen.

Chapter 12: A Paranoid Escape Artist

IT CAN ONLY BE A TESTAMENT TO GOD'S GOODNESS, PROVISION, AND PROMISE that after losing everything we owned in Nicaragua, we were able to start our lives all over again by working hard and saving enough money to buy a $250,000 home in Orange County. He truly did restore to us for the years the swarming locusts had eaten (see Joel 2:25). The plan was to open the doors of our home to the elderly as a convalescent home, starting in 1987. (We never imagined starting a five bed assisted living facility in our own house. But a friend of ours, Mercedes Collins, who owned and administrated a board-and-care-home with her husband, Daniel Collins, encouraged us to do the same.)

For the next 15 years, 25562 Gloriosa Drive would be our new address. In late May, we became the proud owners of a 7,000 square foot lot on which 2,750 square feet was used as a two-story living space. The house featured four-bedrooms with three full bathrooms and an outdoor recreational space made up of a large swimming pool and Jacuzzi. We slept upstairs and the elderly slept downstairs. Kathy was our first female resident and Kurt was our first male resident. Barbara who worked for an elderly placement agency in town referred them to us.

Celebrating Kathy's 70th birthday at our Gloriosa home. Rosi—our first caregiver—helped me make her a special dinner that consisted of ham and cheese appetizers, homemade beef and vegetable lasagna and chocolate cake for dessert. Crystalina is almost 1-year-old. Mission Viejo. 1987.

Kurt was in the later stages of both Alzheimer's and Dementia when we agreed to have him come live with us. Two things about him come to mind: his debilitating paranoia and his uncanny ability to escape our facility. Besides being diagnosed with Alzheimer's and Dementia, Kurt suffered from chronic paranoia. He believed someone was always out to get him. Come the witching-hour, he was inconsolable. Thoughts of delusion clouded his thinking at night. Alone in his room, Kurt armed himself with whatever he could find and began fighting off delusional characters who he thought were dangerous attackers. It got so bad that I moved in with him downstairs and become his roommate for months.

He was also an escape artist. Although his mind didn't always work the way it was supposed to, he had two tremendous virtues, patience and determination, which he used to his advantage as he waited for opportune times to sneak out of our home when someone would carelessly leave the door ajar. Ironically, we became paranoid of his wily escape plans. So we were constantly concerned about our first resident. But even while we relentlessly adapted to his erratic behavior, we continued to care for Kurt. He was not a bad man but a man who suffered greatly during his golden years.

Celebrating our first Christmas at our Gloriosa home. Santa is handing out presents to the elderly. Kurt is receiving a gift from us. Mission Viejo. 1987.

Meeting with Daniel and Mercedes Collins for the first time at a restaurant in Dana Point. They wanted to get to know us better so they invited us to dine with them. (Mercedes is a fellow Nicaragüense.) The idea to start our own assisted living facility was seeded into our hearts this evening. Dana Point. Summer 1985.

Celebrating my 45th birthday at our new home in Mission Viejo. Left to right: Humberto Arguello, me and my first cousin, Ramón Gonzalez. December 21, 1987.

Chapter 13: Glorious Homes Full

WE STARTED CONSTRUCTION DOWNSTAIRS to convert our family room and dining room into semi-private bedrooms for the elderly. Within six months of opening our doors, all our beds were fully occupied with five residents, thanks to Barbara, the owner of an elderly placement agency, as well as Dolores, a kind, business-minded woman, who worked for the state-licensing department.

Although God had provided for us financially, we were constantly working—day and night—caring for all the physical, emotional, and spiritual needs of our residents. This type of works weighs heavily on a person. Since we couldn't afford caregivers, Chester and I became their caregivers, besides handling the business side of things. We split the responsibilities of caregiving. (It wasn't until the next year that we hired the first caregiver, named Rosi, and she was wonderful. She did it all. Glorious Homes was blessed to have an angel like Rosi serve the elderly and our family, incessantly and wholeheartedly.)

In those early days of our business, I did all the laundry and cooking for the elderly, which meant making them breakfast, lunch, and dinner, as well as snacks. I was also responsible for showering and clothing the female residents, not to mention putting on the finishing touches, such as doing their hair and make-up. My dutiful husband was in charge of our male residents' grooming needs. One of the most important care aspects involved dispensing their medication with the right dosage at the right time.

To provide mental and physical activity, we'd offer activities like Bingo, play-set bowling and strolls outdoors. And to provide for their spiritual well being, we'd conduct weekly Bible studies. At least once a week, Chester and I would take our residents to a nice restaurant for a meal out.

Celebrating my 37th birthday in our Gloriosa home with my favorite cake (Carrot Chocolate) and my favorite people. Left to right: Chestercito, Damarita, "Coco," Damaris, me, Victoria holding Ricardito, Orlanda and JP. Mission Viejo. March 13, 1988.

Chestercito holding up the present Damarita gave him for his 15th birthday. We got him a bodybuilding cake because he started competing. Mission Viejo. October 15, 1988.

Celebrating Chester's 46th birthday in the backyard of our Gloriosa home. Chester loved to BBQ! We had just put up the white picket fence (behind us) around the pool because Crystalina was not yet able to swim. Mission Viejo. December 21, 1988.

Chapter 14: Overcoming Stereotypes

OUR LIVES WERE RIDDLED WITH DIFFICULTY AND CHALLENGES. Not only were we entering into a physically and emotionally exhausting business, we were also raising a rebellious teenager—Chester Jr.—and an impressionable pre-teen—Jean Pierre—as well as nursing a newborn—Crystal.

Ideally, with all the daily responsibilities and stresses of our lives, we should've planned to get away—just the two of us—on a more consistent basis. For this season of our lives, however, we were tied to our jobs and children, not to mention the proverbial factor of a limited surplus that comes with starting a new business from scratch. Our family barely had any money left over at the end of the month to spend on leisure activities.

And our reputation as neophyte owners-administrators-caregivers was on the line. As foreigners, who spoke broken English, we faced the challenge of overcoming people's stereotypes about us not being able to communicate with their loved ones in order to provide them with the proper care. When you put all these trials together, you can better appreciate the weight of concern Chester and I experienced on a daily basis. But as we've all experienced, life has its bad days *and* good days.

Chapter 15: ¡Viva Las Vegas!

SIX MONTHS AFTER WE OPENED OUR DOORS TO THE ELDERLY, we started taking them on a yearly excursion to Las Vegas to enjoy the neon-soaked strip with its quintessential casino hotels and restaurants. Our residents loved playing the slot machines and eating prime rib. Our hotel-resort of choice was Circus Circus, which featured free circus acts. I keenly remember the $1 shrimp cocktails and foot long hot dogs. Las Vegas provided a much needed respite from life's daily demands. The main thing that got us through these hard times were our prayers for God's blessings on our family. Without a doubt, I know the Lord had mercy on us because we remembered to care for "widows in their distress" (James 1:27).

Mother's Day at our favorite restaurant, Anthony's Pier. Dana Point Harbor.
Crystalina is 1½-years-old. May 1988.

Circus Circus. Summer 1988.

Chapter 16: Glorious Homes #2

IN THE COMMENCEMENT OF '89, we opened Glorious Homes #2 in Mission Viejo. At this time in our careers, our reputation as conscientious and caring administrators of a board-and-care home began to spread around town like wildfire. There was even a waitlist of people that wanted to have their loved ones in our care. As we began to grow and become more aware of how a business of this type operates, we increased our outings and activities with the elderly. For example, we started taking our residents to a weekly adult day program at Mount of Olives Lutheran Church off La Paz Road. At the time, Chestercito, would join us and call "Big Bingo."

With some of the elderly from Glorious Homes at Mount of Olives Senior Center. Left to right: Chester, Carole, Genieve, me and Ruth. Mission Viejo. Spring 1989.

On the Staten Island Ferry to see the Statue of Liberty with my sister and her boys. Left to right: Martha, Joseph, me, Crystalina and Luis Sterling. Summer 1989.

Celebrating Chester's 47th birthday at our Gloriosa home. Left to right: Doña Coco Silva, me, Chester, Lucho, Mildred and Victoria Porta Campos. Mission Viejo. December 21, 1989.

Crystalina (almost 3) with Daddy on Christmas Day. Mission Viejo. 1989.

Chapter 17: Friends and Family

CONNIE AND HUMBERTO ARGUELLO became an important part of our lives thanks to our nephew José René Delagneau. Connie and José René worked together at the same life insurance company. We would have them over to our house regularly to eat dinner, enjoy some drinks and share some laughs. And in return they invited us to their home to enjoy Humberto's BBQ chicken and steak. On the weekends, we—the Arguellos and the Delagneaus—liked to frequent a restaurant on Mission Viejo Lake, called Tortilla Flats. At times, the Camposes—Dr. José Tomás, Victoria, José Tomás, Ricardo, Alberto, Alfonso, Eduardo and Victoria Isabel—would join us, either at our home or their home.

Then we became fast friends with some other Nicaragüenses—Carla and Eduardo Castro. We loved spending time with our friends and family who brought joy and merriment into our lives.

At Mercedes's home with the Arguellos for dinner and drinks. (Connie Arguello is on the left.) Mission Viejo. 1989.

Chapter 18: A New Decade

WHILE THE '80s WERE KNOWN FOR CONSERVATIVE ECONOMICS (Reaganomics), consumerism and cultural icons made popular by music television (MTV), the '90s can best be described as an era of progress and prosperity ushered in by the '80s booming economy. God willed it and thus we—personally and professionally—benefitted from that economy. And so did the elderly. In this fertile soil of tax reduction and free market activity, the sweat from our brow watered the seed of our mission statement—"Where Love, Personal Care and Dignity are Found." Our elderly residents tasted its fruit.

This was also a time of relative peace. In Nicaragua, the Sandinistan tyranny came to an end on April 25, 1990 when their opposition—Violeta Chamorro—was sworn into office. "The '90s saw Nicaragua's renaissance as the Sandinistas gave in to a fair, popular vote after the fall of the Soviet Bloc."[47]

Holding Myriam. Miguel Soto invited us to his home in Stanton to celebrate the swearing in of the official new President of Nicaragua—Violeta Chamorro. Just as her husband's assassination sparked the Sandinistan Revolution, her election promised an end to the war. April 25, 1990.

---

[47] Alan Arnesto, "Nicaragua," https://chesterdelagneau.com/?p=1266.

It was during this time that Myriam and I began to dream of one day returning to our beloved homeland to visit our family and see for ourselves the destructive rubble left behind by The Sandinistan (Communist) Revolution.

I remember feeling that this new beginning would bring new horizons of growth for all of us, including our children. And it did. Crystalina quickly moved out of her "terrible twos" and into her "magic years" that were dominated by fantasy and a vivid imagination. Jean Pierre graduated from his grammar school—Del Cerro Elementary School. And Chestercito encountered a punctuated growth in his physical development via bodybuilding and wrestling.

Chestercito's first bodybuilding competition called Mr. West Coast with his best friend, Janis Cilderman. Janis took first place and Jr. took second. It was hard to beat Janis. He was tall and well proportioned like Arnold Schwarzenegger, while Chester had a shorter, more compact build like Franco Columbu. Chestercito was a freshman and Janis was a sophomore. Summer 1989.

JP 6th grade at Del Cerro Elementary.
Spring 1990.

Day trip to Mexico with the family. This picture was taken on Avenida Revolución in Tijuana. Crystalina is 3½-years-old.
Summer 1990.

Chestercito's second bodybuilding
competition. This time he took
first place at the North vs. South
Muscle Classic by Manu Pluton
Productions. Fall 1990.

On the front porch of our Gloriosa home. (Myriam's sister, Sylvia, took the picture.) November 1990.

Chapter 19: Busy Bees

YEARS '91 AND '92 PROVED TO BE BUSY ONES FOR THE DELAGNEAUS. Besides celebrating birthdays, holidays, a wedding and a graduation, we started the recovery process of our four properties in Nicaragua. Something we had dreamed about for years was now becoming a reality. We also got a new dog named Cinny. One more thing the Lord blessed us with during this time was opening Glorious Homes #3.

On June 18, 1992, Chestercito graduated from Mission Viejo High School. This was exciting news for many reasons, not least of all because Jr. had been battling learning difficulties brought on by his attention deficit disorder (ADD) for years. He was never diagnosed as a child, so we didn't know why he was having so much trouble learning at school. This exacerbated his undiagnosed anxiety and depression, as well as his obsessive and fearful thoughts. (When he was young, just after we left our war-torn country to arrive in the United States, Chestercito started stuttering and pulling out his hair, a form of Obsessive-Compulsive Disorder (OCD) called Trichotillomania. We didn't understand it at the time. Matter-of-fact, we were very frustrated with him because we thought his disturbing behavior was something he could control. Now we know better.) In retrospect, it makes sense why Chestercito was so moody and rebellious. Thank goodness he had physical exercise to help him release his anger.

Later that summer, I—Myriam—traveled to Nicaragua for the first time since I left there over a decade ago. Chester and I came to an agreement that it would be safer for me to represent our family since the socio-political tension between the Contras and Sandinistas had not yet subsided and he would be more of a target. Also, many members of my family still lived there, such as my sisters (Lina and Fanny) and mother, so I wanted to see them in person. In Managua, I met with a lawyer named Anibal Zuniga who was representing other Nicaragüenses who had lost their property during the war. He agreed to help us reclaim our property in Las Colinas Sur. We had three other homes that needed reclamation but that didn't happen until later with different legal representation.

Picnic with friends in Dana Point: Left to right: Connie, Caesar, Crystalina, me, Mercedes and Yvette. February 1991.

JP celebrating his fourteenth birthday with friends and family in the dinning room of our Gloriosa home. Left to right: Travis, Bunpei, Wayne, Tony, JP, Damarita holding Veronica, Crystalina, me, Auxiliadora Soto and Marcela. June 7, 1991.

Chestercito wrestling for Mission Viejo High School his junior year. This particular match was against an opponent from a rival school, El Toro. Our son dominated the match! Fall 1991.

Chestercito took first place for his division— 13 to 17-year's-old—at the Natural Nationals Mr./Mrs. All American Bodybuilding Competition. September 28, 1991.

Principal Robert Metz shaking Chestercito's hand at Mission Viejo High School's graduation ceremony. June 18, 1992.

With our residents from Glorious Homes #3 at the Elephant Bar Restaurant for lunch. Laguna Hills. Spring 1992.

Dancing at the reception of Victoria Isabel and Danny Meza's wedding.
Cypress Community Center. March 21, 1992.

Victoria Isabel and Danny Meza's wedding party at St. Pius V Catholic Church. Left to right: Tarina, Isabel,
Damarita, bride and groom: Victoria and Danny, Sergio, Alberto and Alfonso; (front) Marcela, Ricardito and
Crystal. Buena Park. March 21, 1992.

Chester in his silk robe showing off his sexy legs on Christmas morning in our living room. Mission Viejo. 1992.

Chapter 20: Honoring Cpl. Rolando A. Delagneau Vivas

NOT EVERYTHING that happened around this time was a blessing to the Delagneaus. Although the civil war in Nicaragua had ended, leaving us physically unscathed, the Gulf War took the life of one of our own—Rolando Delagneau.

Rolando A. Delagneau Vivas was Chester's first cousin. He gave his life serving the United States Army Reserve during the Persian Gulf War in 1991. The war, which lasted about six months (August 2, 1990–February 28, 1991), took the life of Alfredo Delagneau Sander's only son just three days before the war ended.

On February 25, an Iraqi Scud missile broke apart while flying over Dhahran, Saudi Arabia, and the warhead fell on the temporary barracks, killing 29 American soldiers—of which Cpl. Rolando was a part. It was the first night of his first mission. He was 30-years-old.

Cpl. Rolando A. Delagneau Vivas, 477th Trans Co., USAR. 1990.

Chapter 21: Platinum Blond

IN 1993, the hot California sun beat down on us that summer like a judge's gavel dolling out judgment. The kids' sun-kissed faces were evidence that they rarely spent time indoors. Jean Pierre especially took advantage of the sun's bleaching effects while surfing at various surf breaks in South Orange County.

Since junior high school at Los Alisos, JP surfed north of the San Clemente Pier. Then, when he got into high school, he ventured out to Lost Winds, Calafia (San Clemente State Beach) and Trestles (San Onofre State Beach).

That summer the family visited Catalina Island. Unfortunately, I—Myriam—was not able to attend. But I did get to join them on our next excursion to Knott's Berry Farm. The Camposes joined us. José Tomás Campos worked at the Chicken Dinner Restaurant at the time.

JP (16) and Crystalina (6¼) sitting on the stairs at our Gloriosa home after church Easter Sunday. April 11, 1993.

Chestercito (almost 20) holding Crystalina (6½) and JP (16) at Catalina Island. Summer 1993.

Knott's Berry Farm. Left to right: (back) me holding Veronica and Chestercito holding Crystalina; (front) JP, Chester and Victoria Summer 1993.

Chapter 22: Growing Pains

CHANGE, PROGRESS AND GROWTH BECAME THEMATIC ELEMENTS between '94 and '96. Our children were growing older and so were we, not to mention our elderly. Ironically, *change* felt like the most consistent thing in our lives during these fast times in Mission Viejo. But it wasn't just us; the world seemed to spin a little faster with the rise of the World Wide Web and the unprecedented cloning of a sheep called Dolly. Scientists were even hopeful of providing evidence for the existence of life on Mars due to a Martian meteorite. The world was definitely changing and so were the Delagneaus.

Crystalina was 7-years-old and boy-crazy. JP was a sophomore in high school working at Juice Stop. Chestercito turned 21-years-old. He quit his first job at 24 Hour Fitness to work as a Paid-Call Fire Fighter and to wait tables at Bennigan's Restaurant.

In the summer of 1994, I went to Nicaragua for a short trip to start the repossession process of our residential property. A few months after my return, on Monday, October 17, 1994, I received a phone call from my sister, Lina, telling me that our mother had died. Berta Julia Mendieta Flores died due to pneumonia. I flew back to Nicaragua as soon as I received the news. There was a viewing at my mom's house in Managua the day before I arrived.

Horseback riding at 2,237 feet above sea level in Matagalpa. The city is well-known for its low hanging clouds. It was on this trip to Nicaragua that we began reclamation of our stolen property. Summer 1994.

The funeral was held on Thursday in Diriamba where she was born. I arranged for a doctor to embalm the body. I also rented a bus and paid for a driver to escort people to the basilica. Church bells tolled outside while pallbearers carried my mother and her coffin inside. We sang her favorite *coritos* (Spanish worship songs), such as Más Allá del Sol, Somos del Señor and Yo Tengo una Corona Allá en el Cielo. Then we read her favorite Psalm—Psalm 23. Afterward, there was a procession from the church to the cemetery. Inside the coffin, I placed a picture that Crystal drew of my mom with two angels lifting her to heaven. The death of my mother hit me very hard. It left me emotionally exhausted. But a month after she passed away, I had a dream about her that made me happy.

Remembering my mother for the humble, hard-working and honorable woman she was.
Managua. 1969.

I dreamt that my sister, Martha, grabbed my hand and told me, "Myriam, don't cry. Come with me. I'll show you something that'll bring you great joy." Martha took me to a place that I've never seen before. It was a gorgeous garden surrounded by a gate. The door was left ajar. I was amazed at all the fragrant and colorful flowers—smells and colors I've never experienced before. My mother was standing in the midst of the garden wearing the same dress she had on the day of her funeral. I couldn't stop staring at her. She looked healthy and beautiful—full of life. Then she smiled at me. When I woke up, I felt at peace. After 25-years, I still have that image of her in the garden engraved onto my heart. I feel a great comfort knowing that my dear mother is in a better place.

JP's sophomore year before his promenade dance ("prom") with Crystalina (7) by his side. Mission Viejo. 1994.

Chestercito on the rocks in Laguna Beach. 1994.

Celebrating the birthday of one our beloved residents—Carole—at our Gloriosa home. Her niece, Mary, is next to her holding her hand. Left to right: Louisa, Mary, Carole, me, Crystalina and Polly. Mission Viejo. Summer 1994.

José René and Gloria's wedding at Las Sierritas de Santo Domingo Church. Managua. November 4, 1995.

Celebrating my 45th birthday with my amor in the formal dinning room of our Gloriosa home. March 13, 1996.

Laguna Beach. 1995.

Senior picture. 1996.

Vice principal shaking JP's hand at Mission Viejo High School's graduation ceremony. June 20, 1996.

Family photo at José's house. Left to right: me, Martin, Lixio, Quincha, Chimba, José and Lucho. New Orleans. November 28, 1996.

At José Tomás's Ave Deseo home for Christmas. José René and Gloria visiting from Nicaragua. Marcela (7) and Veronica (6) are in the fore. Mission Viejo. 1996.

Chapter 23: Church Bells Chime

THE DAY AFTER VALENTINE'S DAY Alberto Campos and Kathy Bliss tied the knot at St. Bartholomew Church in Long Beach. We were so excited to be at the wedding to celebrate the sacred union of these two wonderful human beings. Alberto, Chester's third cousin, is a gifted musician and drummer, and Kathy is the kindest, most thoughtful person we've ever known. So naturally we wanted to be there.

Weddings are the most joyful of occasions. To see a man and woman enter into a covenant of marriage before friends, family and God as they proclaim their forever love to one another is always inspiring. I remember this special day as being the epitome of just that. As an added bonus, I got to see my own children get dressed up. I remember taking a picture of Chester teaching Jr. how to tie a tie for the first time. What a blessed day!

Chester helping Jr. with his tie for the wedding. Mission Viejo. February 15, 1997.

Outside St. Bartholomew Church after the ceremony. Long Beach. 1997.

Left to right: Chestercito, Damaris, me, Crystalina and JP. St. Bartholomew Church. 1997.

Cabrillo Beach break one week after JP's 20th birthday. June 14, 1997.

Chapter 24: Salvation

CHESTERCITO AND HIS FRIENDS—John and Benir—took a trip early June in '98 across the Atlantic Ocean. For a month, they backpacked all over Western Europe, travelling to England, Netherlands, Switzerland, France, Spain, Italy and Greece. Our son was desperately seeking something, anything to fill the void of discontentment in his life. God was simultaneously showing him the beauty and wonder of His creation while calling him to Himself. But first Chestercito would have to be broken.

When Jr. returned from living carefree and carelessly across the world as a prodigal son, God got a hold of his heart in the form of heartbreak. It was devastating to watch. He needed spiritual and psychological support, and he needed it fast. On July 21, 1998, our firstborn son surrendered his life to following our Lord Jesus Christ as his personal Savior. Our son would never be the same again. He stopped hanging out with his old friends and started a Bible study at our Gloriosa home. His best friend to date—Neal Caldwell—was a part of that tight group of young Christians who met regularly in our living room.

Because of their friendship, Chestercito started working as a summer camp counselor with Neal at the school where Neal taught physical education. Our son also started working as the Activities Director at our board-and-care homes for the elderly. Needless to say, this was not the same Chestercito from before. Our prayers had been answered. He was a new and improved man—a man of God on a spiritual journey of shedding his old life of sin and suffering and putting on a new life of peace, purpose and power.[48]

Chestercito and Benir at the top of the Eiffel Tower. France. June 1998.

---

[48] To read more about Chestercito's testimony, please visit his blog at https://chesterdelagneau.com.

Chestercito and Benir at the Colosseum in Rome. June 1998.

Chestercito, John and Benir in front of St. Peter's Basilica in Vatican City. Rome. June 1998.

Chapter 25: Endless Summer

In line for a Kaanapali Luau at our Marriott Hotel. Maui. July 1998.

WHEN CHESTERCITO RETURNED FROM EUROPE, we left as a family to Hawaii followed by Nicaragua, Costa Rica and then Mexico. It felt like an endless summer. We had never been to Hawaii before so it was a big deal that we were all going together. Of course, we did all the touristy stuff in Maui, like taking the scenic drive on the highway to Hana, snorkeling in Kaanapali, parasailing, cliff jumping, attending a luau, and going to too many touristy restaurants. We spent a week in Hawaii but it felt like we were there the whole summer.

Chestercito and JP eating at a Kaanapali luau on the beach of our hotel. Maui. July 1998.

In Kaanapali returning from the market. Maui. July 1998.

Then we traveled to Nicaragua, our first time as a whole family. For over a week we stayed at José René and Gloria's home in Managua, which they converted into a chateau, called Chateau Delagneau. It was intended to attract high-end clientele, such as political dignitaries. We scheduled fun excursions to Masaya, Montelimar and the Playas de Pochomil. We even attended the annual parade honoring the Managuan Patron Saint—Santo Domingo.

Pochomil Beach. Left to right: (back) Chestercito and JP; (front) Mercedes holding Celeste, Crystalina and Nicole. Nicaragua. August 1998.

Horseback riding in Las Playas de Pochomil. Nicaragua. August 1998.

Costa Rica was our next destination. We stayed with my cousin, Nilda Martha Porta Caldera, for a few days. We happened to be there the same time as Nilda and Damaris's mother's (Doña Teresita's) 80th birthday. There, in San José, we enjoyed being tourists all around town. I remember it rained for the majority of our trip.

From there, we came home for a few days before we left for our final trip of the summer. We headed south to Rosarito Beach, Mexico. For a week, we walked the coast in the mornings to buy fresh produce. Then, in the afternoons, we drove to Tijuana to walk Avenida Revolución to purchase souvenirs and pan dulce (sweet bread). In the evenings, we liked to eat dinner at Los Arcos Restaurant, well-known for their seafood.

Rosarito. August·1998.

Glorious Homes #2, our resident—Georgia—blowing out her candles to her birthday cake. She turned 100-years-old. Left to right: Myriam, Mabel, Georgia, Hazel, Chestercito and me. Mission Viejo. End of summer 1998.

Chestercito dancing with Natalie—another resident—at Georgia's birthday party. Mission Viejo. End of summer 1998.

Los Angeles County Arboretum and Botanic Garden. Arcadia. Fall 1998.

Chapter 26: "Party Like It's 1999!"

WE DELAGNEAUS LOVE TO PARTY. And in 1999, there were a lot of things to celebrate: Chestercito was rockin' his role as Glorious Homes' Activity Director (literally, he was playing worship songs on his guitar as part of the elderlies' spiritual enrichment); our facilities participated in the annual Walk to End Alzheimer's sponsored by the Alzheimer's Association; Chestercito and Crystalina were water-baptized at Saddleback Church Lake Forest; Crystalina received the volleyball award for Best Server at Saddleback Valley Christian School; Cinny—our sheltie-collie mix that we got from an animal rescue shelter—lived out the rest of her life with us that year; and we enjoyed the weddings of a close friend and family member.

Chestercito being baptized at Saddleback Church Lake Forest. February 14, 1999.

Chestercito playing guitar for the elderly at Glorious Homes #2. Spring 1999.

Baptism party at our Gloriosa home. I had a seamstress make a
beautiful dress for Crystalina. Summer 1999.

Proudly representing Glorious Homes at the Walk to End Alzheimer's. Irvine Spectrum. October 1999.

JP congratulating Crystalina after her outstanding performance in volleyball
against Saddleback Valley Christian rival—St. Margaret's.
San Juan Capistrano. October 1999.

Chestercito and JP in the backyard gazebo of our Gloriosa home before Juan Carlos's wedding. November 1999.

Backyard gazebo before Alfonso and Tarina's wedding. November 1999.

Fall of 1999.

I commissioned this portrait of me to my cousin, Amilcar Mendieta.

Holding Tommy Boy on my lap as I caress Cinny to my right. Cinny died later that year of lymphatic cancer. We loved her to the best of our ability until she was no longer in any pain. Winter 1999.

Annual Glorious Homes' Christmas party at facility #3 with Chestercito playing Santa. 1999.

Chapter 27: A New Hope, A New Decade, A New Century

IN THE YEAR 2000, GOD BEGAN A NEW WORK IN OUR LIVES. Myriam and I knew that we wanted to move from Mission Viejo to be closer to the ocean. So we started scouting Dana Point and San Clemente for places to live. Chestercito was finishing up his Associate of Arts degree at Saddleback College to transfer to Azusa Pacific University the following year. He also became impassioned with Christian apologetics—a branch of theology that rationally defends itself from objections to the Christian faith. JP moved out to live in Newport Beach and to work in sales for a clothing company called Johnny Suede. Crystalina began junior high at Saddleback Valley Christian School in San Juan Capistrano. And we got a new dog—Cassidy.

One sad thing that happened at the end of Y2K is the passing of my mother, whom I loved and treasured dearly. She died November 1, 2000 of pulmonary fibrosis. She meant everything to me; she was my garrison of strength and incarnation of kindness. She will be forever my Lixio and I will be forever her Chaleoncito.

Chestercito's graduation ceremony at Saddleback College with Marcela, Veronica, Damarita and Crystalina. May 18, 2001.

Crystalina in her 8th grade Saddleback Valley Christian School graduation regalia. June 2001.

With my beloved, singing karaoke at my brother's house one day before Leslie's wedding. Metairie. June 29, 2001.

Leslie's wedding reception at Crystal Palace. Left to right: (back) Chestercito, José, José Tomás, Lucho and Eddie; (front) Martin, JP, Leslie, me, Charlie and his father. New Orleans. June 30, 2001.

Mildred's house the day after Leslie's wedding. Left to right: (back) José, Chester and Mildred; (front) Ruby, Lixio and Rosa Lila. Metairie. July 1, 2001.

With Myriam at Fisherman's Restaurant scouting San Clemente. We were renting a place for two months (June-July) in Laguna Niguel before we moved into our new home in San Clemente in the beginning of September. July 2001.

Our new home. 1800 Avenida Salvador. San Clemente. Picture taken 2006.

Chapter 28: Radical Islamic Jihadists

I—MYRIAM—REMEMBER HEARING THE NEWS TUESDAY MORNING of terrorist attacks on United States' soil. I called my son, who was living in Azusa renting an apartment off-campus; he had not yet heard the harrowing news. With deep sadness, I told him what had just happened: Al-Qaeda—a radical Islamic group—coordinated a series of terrorist attacks via hijacking four commercial airline planes: the first crashed into the North Tower of the World Trade Center (WTC) in New York City; the second crashed into the South Tower of WTC; the third hit the Pentagon in Virginia; and the last plane never reached its suspected destination of Washington, D.C., due to the heroic efforts of passengers that caused the plane to crash land in a field near Shanksville, Pennsylvania. Besides costing billions of dollars in infrastructure and property damage, 9/11 was the single deadliest terrorist attack in human history. In total, nearly 3,000 people were killed and over 25,000 were injured.

What I remember most about 9/11 is the aftermath: first responders and peace officers risked their lives at ground zero to rescue those injured and trapped under rubble. The American people united themselves under the banner of prayer. Political differences seemed to diminish during this time of national insecurity. For a short time it seemed like there was no separation of church and state. We were all hungry for peace, unity and restoration. The slogan "We will never forget" was our mourning cry. But soon thereafter, people did forget, maybe not the evil of 9/11 but the good.

Personally, the terrorist attack in New York hit a little too close to home for me since it was the first place I visited in the United States and because I have family who live there. My sister, Martha, lived in Manhattan and worked for New York City, and her sons, Luis and Joseph, lived in the Bronx.

Statue of Liberty and Twin Towers. This picture was taken prior to the destruction of the Twin Towers on 9/11. Photo courtesy of Shutterstock. By Benny Marty.

Stature of Liberty and Twin Towers. This picture was taken during the destruction of the Twin Towers on 9/11. By US National Park Service employee, https://commons.wikimedia.org/wiki/File:National_Park_Service_9-11_Statue_of_Liberty_and_WTC.jpg. Adapted to black and white.

Chapter 29: Never Lose Faith

MIXED EMOTIONS is the best way to describe how we felt during the years 2002-2004. On Easter Sunday, April 11, 2003, my sister, Rosa Lila, died. She was survived by her loving husband, Edwin "Eddie" Blais, and their two children, Jared and Leslie. In the last year-and-a-half of her life, Rosa Lila suffered from amyotrophic lateral sclerosis (ALS), commonly referred to as Lou Gehrig's Disease, which degenerates nerve cells weakening muscles and compromising physical function. In her case, the disease started with her throat, leaving her unable to talk. What was most remarkable about my sister is that she never lost faith even as her body broke down, affecting her ability to breathe and swallow on her own. This was painful for her to endure and for those around her to witness. We miss her greatly. But we're comforted knowing that we'll see her again in the arms of our loving, heavenly Father.

A couple months later, I had a complete hip replacement due to the constant shock my hips had absorbed while parachute training during my days in the military. This was a difficult season in my life. But I knew I had to get better fast in order to take care of my family. The recent memory of my dear sister motivated me to stay positive and be thankful for what I have.

I chose this picture of Rosa Lila and Eddie's wedding by which to honor her. I know that that day was the happiest of her life next to the birth of her son and daughter. December 7, 1963.

Chapter 30: Nicaraguan and Norwegian Worlds Collide

CREATIVE WRITING HAD BECOME CHESTERCITO'S PASSION. For a change of scenery, he would frequent Starbucks in downtown San Clemente to work on his speculative fiction novel, titled *Salvador*. It was November 2003, and little did I—Myriam—know that during the month of Thanksgiving I would soon have even more to be thankful for. After asking the Lord for three decades for a God-fearing woman for my son, my prayers were answered. Her name was Sari Merritt. Turns out, she too frequented Starbucks, in her case, to complete coursework for her teaching credential. After a mutual friend made introductions, it ignited a spark of friendship. It would be another few months before Chestercito mustered the courage to ask Sari on a date.

On February 26, 2004, they went on their first date to Gen Kai Sushi. Six months later, they got engaged and a year to the day of their first date, they were married. So, on February 26, 2005, she became Sari Delagneau. She comes from a Norwegian paternal background and Scottish maternal background. Her parents are Bible-believing Christians. She comes from good stock.

Chestercito and Sari met at Starbucks in San Clemente, went on their first date in Dana Point, got engaged at the Montage Resort in Laguna Beach, were married at South Coast Christian Assembly in San Juan Capistrano, danced all night at their reception at Del Agave in San Clemente and honeymooned in Saint Lucia.

Chestercito and Sari dancing at Adrian and Rachel's wedding at the Ole Hanson Beach Club one day after Chestercito and Sari got engaged. San Clemente. August 27, 2004.

At North Beach in San Clemente. Early February 2005.

South Coast Christian Assembly. San Juan Capistrano. February 26, 2005.

Chestercito and Sari's wedding reception at Del Agave. San Clemente. February 26, 2005.

Sylvia and I at Chestercito and Sari's wedding. San Juan Capistrano. February 26, 2005.

Luis, Joseph and Sylvia with the bride-and-groom. February 26, 2005.

Mother-Son Dance at Chestercito's wedding. I remember we
danced to my favorite instrumental song "Ballade pour Adeline"
by Richard Clayderman. February 26, 2005.

Chapter 31: Hurricane Katrina: Bursting New Orleans's Levees

WITH UNPRECEDENTED FEROCITY AND DEVASTATION, HURRICANE KATRINA struck on August 26, 2005. Moving westward from Florida, Katrina emerged as a Category 5 hurricane over the warm waters of the Gulf of Mexico. It weakened to a Category 3 as it made landfall over southeast Louisiana. As a result of fatal engineering flaws in flood protection known as levees, which surround the city of New Orleans, 80% of the city was flooded for weeks. Transportation systems were destroyed leaving thousands and thousands of people stranded with little to no access to food and/or shelter. Thankfully, none of our family members was directly affected by the flood. Sadly, the Catholic school where Chestercito and JP attended, when we lived in New Orleans, as well as our favorite eatery—Liuzza's—was flooded.

But what stands out most to me about Hurricane Katrina is the disaster relief efforts made by federal, local and private organizations. Federal Emergency Management Agency (FEMA) and the United States Coast Guard (USCG) are but two federal government agencies that responded. Even international governments, such as France, Germany and Mexico, volunteered to help. Our church (Saddleback Church), as part of its Peace Disaster Relief, set up a holistic plan to combat the destruction of Katrina and other disasters. Pastor Rick Warren, the founding and senior pastor of Saddleback, calls these efforts R.E.L.I.E.F. This acrostic stands for **R**ally our small groups; **E**ngage local churches as relief centers; **L**ink with public and private partners; **I**nclude physical, emotional, and spiritual support; **E**mpower survivors to help each other; and **F**und what's overlooked.[49]

Natural disasters, such as Katrina, and man-made disasters, such as 9/11, will always have greater foes, such as the efforts of the church and people working together for the dignity and flourishing of all human beings.

Liuzza's inundated by Hurricane Katrina. September 2005.

---

[49] The Christian Post, "How Saddleback Spells Relief," Online by Rick Warren, CP Guest Contributor, https://www.christianpost.com/news/how-saddleback-spells-r-e-l-i-e-f.html (accessed July 18, 2020).

Chestercito and JP at Holy Rosary Catholic School circa early 1980s. They attended this school for several years until we moved to California. Hurricane Katrina inundated the school some 40 years later.

Chapter 32: Zela Ursulina "Lina"

SOMETIMES THE DEATH OF ONE TRAGEDY IS THE BIRTH OF ANOTHER. In 2005, Hurricane Katrina hit our former place of residence quite hard. Then, in 2006, death knocked yet again too close to home. My sister, Zela Ursulina "Lina" Mendieta De Garcia died May 8, 2006 from colon cancer. But I'd like to remember Lina by telling a story that involves her selfless act of helping us reclaim our property in Nicaragua.

When I'd arrived in Managua in 1994 to meet with a lawyer about repossessing our home, I was told that a Russian family was renting the property we were seeking to reclaim. While I was there, I remembered a kind, elderly woman who lived down the street from our home. So I paid her a visit. And after all these years, she was still alive and she remembered me. As it turned out, her son spoke Russian and, although he was a Sandinista, he was willing to help us. (He remembered my kindness to him and his family as a child when I'd given him clothes and a bicycle.) He spoke to the Russian family and told them we had our home stolen from us by the Sandinistas during the Revolution. The family empathized and sympathized with us. Moreover, they were willing to move out so we could move in. We made plans to have my sister, Lina, and her son, José Félix, and his wife, Maria Esperanza Matuz, occupy the space right away. Feeling elated, I flew back home the same day.

A couple of days later, Lina called with the heartbreaking news that a mob of heavily armed Sandinistas broke into the house and threw them out. They weren't allowed to take anything with them. So, they lost their personal belongings and we lost our home, yet again.

Twelve years later, while living in San Clemente, I received a phone call that Lina had passed away. She hadn't wanted her family to know she'd been suffering from cancer, not wanting to burden us. I found out the truth through a close friend of hers. Her sister-in-law, Anita Garcia De Gomez, had the viewing and funeral in her own home followed by the procession to church and then to the cemetery. Lina was survived by her four daughters, Maria Eugenia, Marcia, Ernestina, Luz Maria, and a son, José Félix.

LA PRENSA

Managua, Sábado 18 de Junio de 1994

Turbas reaparecen defendiendo la "piñata"

Desalojo con violencia en Las Colinas

CELSO CANELO CANDIA

Doña Zela Mendieta Mendieta denunció ante LA PRENSA que con lujo de violencia y prepotencia, el subcomandante Francisco Ramírez, acompañado de 20 hombres bien armados la desalojaron de su casa número 44 que está ubicada en la zona residencial Las Colinas.

Explicó la denunciante que a raíz del triunfo de los sandinistas, éstos le quitaron la casa a su hermana Miriam Mendieta, quien es la legítima dueña de la propiedad, pero después se posesionó de la residencia la señora María Esther Sequeira y su esposo Enrique Vega Lacayo.

Agregó que después que los sandinistas perdieron el poder en enero de 1990, María Esther Sequeira se "piñateó", la casa y la alquiló al señor Damir Ewdokimov, de origen soviético quien arrendaba la casa en 1,500 dólares mensual.

"Después de una serie de gestiones judiciales que hice para recuperar la casa de mi hermana, el señor Ewdokimov me la entregó el miércoles pasado de forma pacífica, pero cual fue mi susto cuando a las diez de la noche del jueves se aparecieron como 20 hombres bien armados a sacarnos de la casa", relató Zela Mendieta.

La señora Mendieta afirmó que los hombres que llegaron a desalojarla de su casa, bajo el mando del subcomandante Francisco Ramírez, rompieron las verjas de la entrada principal de la residencia y las puertas del garaje.

"El subcomandante Ramírez me amenazó de muerte y dijo que si no salía de la casa toda mi familia iba a perecer. Yo le respondí que cómo se atrevían entrar con violencia a mi propia casa, que eran unos sinvergüenzas, piñateros", relató doña Zela Mendieta.

En tanto, José Félix García Mendieta, hijo de doña Zela Mendieta, manifestó que tres hombres con revólver en mano le "echaron una llave" y lo sacaron de arrastras de la casa.

Agregó que los individuos llegaron en tres vehículos, una kuzuca blanca MH-1478, un carro Toyota color gris, placas número MP-5941, y el subcomandante Ramírez llegó en una camioneta Toyota color rojo, placa CMK 5902.

La familia Mendieta informó que ayer esperaron al Juez Cuarto de Distrito de lo Civil de Managua, doctor Encarnación Castañeda Miranda, para que acompañado del abogado, doctor Aníbal Zúniga, procedieran a desalojar "a un grupo de turbas que mantienen tomada la vivienda".

Doña Zela Mendieta manifestó

Pasa a la P-12

195

Desalojo

que después que los 20 hombres la desalojaron la noche del jueves, ayer por la mañana la casa apareció tomada por un grupo de "turbas sandinistas", que se encuentran "armados hasta lo dientes".

"Yo espero que se haga justicia y que me sea devuelta la casa, además denunciaré ante los derechos humanos de Nicaragua y del exterior el ultraje que recibí de un alto militar sandinista", externó Mendieta.

Al mismo tiempo, aseguró que seguirá luchando hasta recuperar su casa que le costó sudor y lágrima a su hermana, Miriam Mendieta, quien reside actualmente en los Estados Unidos.

Por vía telefónica, la señora Miriam Mendieta llamó desde San Francisco California a LA PRENSA, para solicitar que se le diera cobertura periodística a su caso.

La Prensa newspaper reporting the violent eviction of my sister, Lina, and her family from our home in Las Colinas at the hands of 20 heavily armed men under the command of Sandinistan Francisco Ramírez. They threatened my family at gunpoint and three men physically assaulted Lina's son, José Félix. Managua. Saturday, June 18, 1994.

Our home, casa #44 de Las Colinas.

Doña Zela Mendieta relata la forma en que un grupo de 20 hombres bien armados, al mando del subcomandante Francisco Ramírez, la llegaron a desalojar de su propia casa ubicada en Las Colinas. En la parte superior de la gráfica, la residencia de la familia Mendieta, que se encuentra tomada por un "grupo de turbas sandinistas", dijo la denunciante.

Lina, on the floor of a neighbor's home pleading for justice after "desalojo con violencia" ("eviction with violence").

Family in Nicaragua. Left to right: (back) JP, William and Chestercito; (front) Fanny, Crystalina, (front of Crystalina) Amy, Lina, Maria Esperanza and me. Managua. August 1998.

Chapter 33: "First Comes Love, Then Comes Marriage..."

MY LONG-TIME PRAYER THAT MY SONS WOULD BE BLESSED with loving, godly women, was answered once more, this time for my son, JP. Priscilla Sarai Sanchez came into his life in the beginning of 2007. With her warmth, affection and kind heart, she fit right into our family fold. Priscilla's caring nature was put further on display when she and JP began to assist us at Glorious Homes, Inc.,[50] in the spring of 2009. Soon, they were operating facility #2 (24672 Argus Drive) and we operated facility #3 (24726 Argus Drive) both in Mission Viejo.

Cabo San Lucas, Mexico, proved the ideal location for JP's proposal in July of 2012. Our son, Chestercito, beautifully performed their wedding ceremony on November 9, 2012, at the El Adobe Restaurant in San Juan Capistrano. What fun we had dancing the night away in celebration of their joyous union.

JP and Priscilla at Chronic Cantina. Newport Beach. January 2007.

---

[50] Glorious Homes was incorporated on June 22, 2004.

JP and Priscilla for JP's 30th birthday at our Salvador home. San Clemente. June 7, 2007.

JP and Priscilla's engagement. Photographed by Ernesto Olivares Photography. July 2012.

JP and Priscilla's engagement. Photographed by Ernesto Olivares Photography.
July 2012.

JP and Priscilla being "clapped in" to their wedding reception at El Adobe de Capistrano. San Juan Capistrano. November 9, 2012.

El Adobe de Capistrano. November 9, 2012.

JP at The Fisherman's Restaurant (bar side) with their first resident, Nina. June 30, 2011.

JP at Facility #2 with their resident, Dorothy. St. Patrick's Day. March 2013.

Chapter 34: A Military Funeral

"UNCLE EDDIE" AS OUR KIDS CALLED HIM went to be with the Lord on Friday, June 22, 2007 after complications with Type 2 Diabetes. Everyone else called him "Chimba"—a name my brother called him forty years ago. That Friday was a tough day for our family, as well as those special people who knew him best and loved him dearly. Myriam and I weren't able to attend the funeral in New Orleans, so Chestercito and JP went to represent the family. Having served in the United States Navy for three years as an aviation electrician, Eddie received a military funeral at St. Louis Cemetery #3, eulogized by his pastor, Rusty Tardo.

We'll never forget Chimba's sense of humor, love of good food, love for his children, love for Jesus and his love for life. The two things that stand out the most to me about Chimba was the way he adored his wife, Rosa Lila (my sister), and the way he showered us with kindness when we came to the United States from Nicaragua.

Eddie (right) enlisted in the US Navy in 1959. He and his brother, Bob, were assigned to VA-56—a jet attack squadron—attached to CVA-14 USS Ticonderoga. In this picture, the USS Ticonderoga was docked either in San Diego or Japan.

Pastor Rusty Tardo giving the eulogy at Eddie's funeral. St. Louis Cemetery #3. New Orleans. June 2007.

Chapter 35: Miss Nicaragua

CRYSTAL WAS SELECTED TO REPRESENT NICARAGUA AS MISS NICARAGUA at Fiestas Patrias ("Patriotic Holidays" that commemorate the independence of Central American countries) organized by Con Feca on Sunday, September 16, 2007 in Los Angeles. (Technically, Nicaragua's Independence Day is on September 15th). That Sabbath consisted of driving up to Los Angeles early morning to have our convertible Mercedes Benz detailed with Nicaraguan paraphernalia: from flags to flowers. Once our car was decorated, we drove in a procession of vehicles behind the Nicaraguan float on which Crystal stood and waved to the crowd of nearly 80,000 spectators at MacArthur Park. This special event consisted of Central American food, music and dancing.

Prior to the festival, there was a ceremony in downtown Los Angeles where the former Miss Nicaragua relinquished her crown to Crystal, who was then crowned Miss Nicaragua 2007. She was also decorated with a banner inscribed with "Srta. Nicaragua 2007," which she donned across her torso over an elegant black dress. A beautiful bouquet of flowers were presented to her, as well.

After the festival, Crystal appeared on ¡Despierta América!, a Spanish morning television show airing on Univision. She was interviewed by the host, who asked her personal questions, such as where she and her family were born, how often she visits Nicaragua, and how much she loves Nicaragua. Crystal's reign as Miss Nicaragua was a time we'll never forget.

We want to express our gratitude to Olga Reñasco Mendieta and Martha Abea for giving Crystal an opportunity to interview and prove herself as Miss Nicaragua 2007.

Crystal as "Miss Nicaragua" standing on the Nicaraguan float with a representative of Goya. MacArthur Park. Los Angeles. September 16, 2007.

"Miss Nicaragua" standing on the Nicaraguan float holding the Nicaraguan flag. MacArthur Park. Los Angeles. September 16, 2007.

Crowned "Miss Nicaragua" downtown Los Angeles.
Early September 2007.

Chapter 36: "Gift from God"

OUR FIRST GRANDCHILD—NATHANAEL JOSEPH DELAGNEAU—was born on March 5, 2009 at Saddleback Medical Center in Laguna Hills, California. Chestercito and Sari's first offspring was named "Nathanael" because of the biblical reference to the Hebrew prophet in the Old Testament and Christ's disciple in the New. His name means "gift from God."

Grandparents share a special bond with their grandchildren just like Jedis share a special bond with their Padawans. The Jedi loves to teach and mold the Padawan; and, in return, the Padawan enjoys the attention. The same goes for grandparents and grandchildren. We feel blessed to share our wisdom and experience with our young Padawan.

Nathanael is an intelligent, creative and passionate young man, who wants to know "Why" things are the way they are. We know God has an amazing plan for his life. Our prayer is that he would use his spiritual gifts and natural abilities to glorify his heavenly Father. We are blessed that he'll continue the legacy of love that we've shown him all the days of his life.

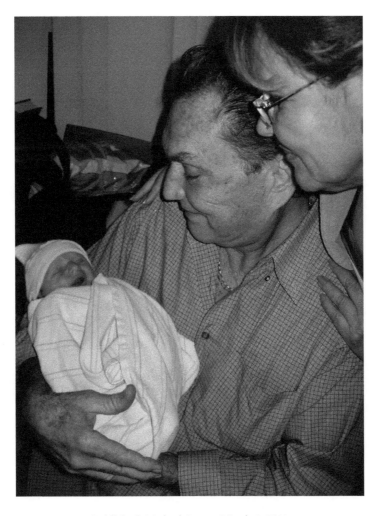

Saddleback Medical Center. March 5, 2009.

Sari holding Nathanael at our Salvador home.
March 8, 2009.

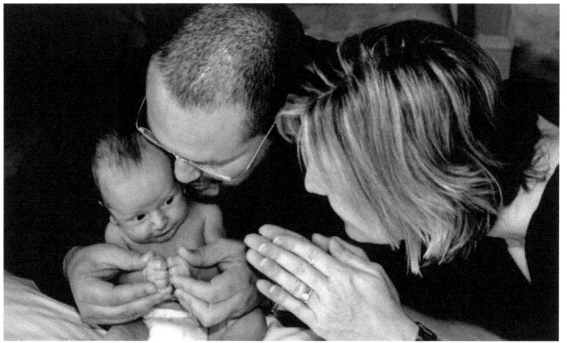

Teaching Nathanael to pray at our Salvador home. March 28, 2009.

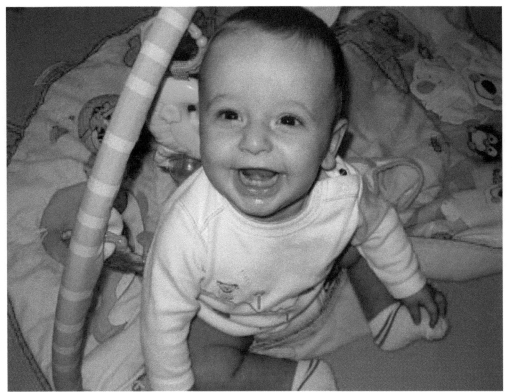

Nathanael's first two teeth came in at six months. September 2009.

Christmas elf at our annual work Christmas party. Mission Viejo. 2010.

Nathanael wearing the "Nicaragua" t-shirt Myriam brought back for him. He's trying not to smile like the picture in the book. San Clemente. Spring 2011.

Celebrating Mother's Day with our beloved grandson. May 2013.

Talega Life Church Preschool. San Clemente. September 9, 2013.

At Chestercito's 40th birthday party. The party's theme was
1940s Big Band and Swing Era. October 2013.

Christmas morning at our Salvador home. 2013.

Fall 2015.

Nathanael enjoying one of my *nacatamales* at our Salvador home. Christmas 2015.

This was Nathanael's fourth year playing for the American Youth Soccer Organization (AYSO). His team name was the Fighting Leprechauns. Nathanael was the leading scorer on his team. September 9, 2018.

Nathanael skating at Ralph's Skate Park on his 11th birthday. San Clemente. March 5, 2020.

Chapter 37: Prostate Cancer

WITH ALL THAT I'VE EXPERIENCED IN MY LIFE, I've learned to never take things for granted, for life can change in an instant. In October 2010, I was admitted to Saddleback Memorial Hospital to get my entire prostate removed. I had blood work done two years prior—at 66-years-old—that showed an abnormally high level of prostate-specific antigen (PSA), which is indicative of prostate cancer. But I wasn't comfortable, at the time, conceding to a prostatectomy. So I waited. By 2010, I knew I didn't want the alternative—chemotherapy—and the possibility of the cancer coming back, so I chose drastic measures to insure that I'd be cancer free after the prostatectomy. I feel blessed with my decision.

My older brother, José, was not as fortunate. He died of prostate cancer on June 12, 2017.

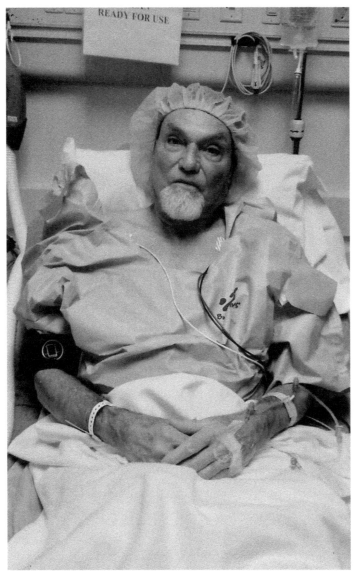

Before surgery. Saddleback Memorial Hospital. October 2010.

Chapter 38: National Certified Medical Assistant (NCMA)

OUR PRECIOUS CRYSTALINA has always had a caring and nurturing heart. We were thrilled when she informed us that she wanted to go into the medical field. In September 2011, Crystal started her educational path toward becoming a certified medical assistant. She graduated a year later through Kaplan University in Escondido. Being there to celebrate and enjoy the fruit of Crystal's labor was the highlight of our year. She went on to take the countrywide exam to become a National Certified Medical Assistant (NCMA).

Afterward, Crystal became an intern for Cordova Medical Group. The doctor noticed Crystal's work ethic and kind bedside manner and immediately hired her. Her clinical and clerical job descriptions consisted of taking patient's vital signs, giving injections, performing wound care, administering EKGs, as well as verifying insurance information and updating medical records.

Chapter 39: Chester Delagneau, B.A., M.A., M.A.

AFTER GRADUATING IN 2005 WITH A BACHELOR'S DEGREE in Human Development (sociology–psychology) from Azusa Pacific University, Chestercito continued his academic education amassing two master's degrees: one in Theology (2009), the other in Philosophy (2011) from Biola's graduate program—Talbot School of Theology. With prayer and Sari's support, Chestercito enrolled and was accepted into Fuller Theological Seminary's Center for Advanced Theological Studies (CATS) in Systematic Theology. However, three years into the Ph.D. program, Chestercito fell ill and was unable to continue his postgraduate research.

It was a long road to recovery for our son but he persevered. And through his "dark night of the soul" (St. John of the Cross), Chestercito came out of it with more compassion and understanding for human suffering than ever before.

Talbot of School of Theology's baccalaureate celebration. Chestercito was hooded and commissioned into ministry. Mildred and Lucho were in attendance. Knott's Berry Farm Hotel. Buena Park. May 26, 2011.

Chestercito's graduation from the Philosophy of Religion and Ethics program at Talbot School of Theology. June 2011.

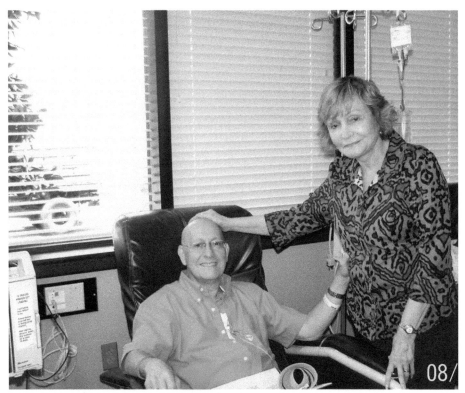

First chemo treatment to battle lymphoma in his lung. August 7, 2011.

Lucho always remained optimistic during his battle with cancer. August 7, 2011.

Chapter 40: Mariann and Martha

MY BEST FRIEND—MARIANN ARREDONDO—GOT ME THROUGH my sister's death. She's always there when I need someone to talk to or pray with. I feel blessed to have a best friend like Mariann to walk with me and hold my hand through life's darkest days.

My eldest sibling, Martha Sterling-Chajet, who was living in Florida at the time, died unexpectedly on September 14, 2012. The conditions surrounding her death are too painful for me to talk about. She was survived by her husband, Dr. George Chajet, and her two sons, Luis and Joseph Sterling.

What I remember most about my sister is her intrepid spirit. At a young age—19-years-old—she left our small town in Nicaragua to make it in the Big Apple. She was also passionate and generous. Martha loved culture, travel and education, but she loved her family most of all. She was also there for my family when we needed financial assistance in the recovery of our homes in Nicaragua.

My sister, Martha, in her late 40s in New York.

At Mozambique restaurant with Mariann and Dan Arredondo, enjoying dinner and drinks while listening to their son, Adam, play Reggae music. Laguna Beach. Summer 2012.

Chapter 41: "...And Then Comes a Baby in a Baby Carriage"

OUR FIRST GRANDDAUGHTER—CAMILA ELIZABETH DELAGNEAU—was born Sunday evening on September 14, 2014 weighing 6 lb, 2 oz at Hoag Hospital in Newport Beach. Chester and I were in New Orleans at the time visiting family. We arrived back in South Orange County a day later. We drove straight from the airport to the hospital to see our healthy, beautiful granddaughter. God blessed our family again with another gift from God.

JP and his Princess. Laguna Niguel. September 20, 2014.

Camilita with her Wubbanub pink bear pacifier.
Laguna Niguel. February 2015.

Nathanael holding Camilita after she was dedicated at Saddleback
Church Lake Forest. Valentine's Day. 2015.

Camilita visiting her "Tita" and Grandpa—
Priscilla's mother and father. Costa Mesa. April 29, 2015.

Camilita's 1st birthday at the park. Laguna Niguel. September 26, 2015.

Fall Fest at Saddleback Church San Clemente. October 25, 2015.

Camilita's 2nd birthday party at the park. Laguna Niguel.
September 13, 2016.

Camilita at the park taking birthday pictures. Turning 3-years-old.
Laguna Niguel. September 13, 2017.

Camilita at the park taking birthday pictures. Turning 5-years-old. Laguna Niguel. September 12, 2019.

Chapter 42: Remembering Martin Hinzie and Luis Sevilla

MARTIN HINZIE AND LUIS SEVILLA were not blood related, but they were brothers-in-law due to the fact they married sisters, Ruby and Mildred. They also shared in common career success in their adopted country.

Martin originated from Guatemala and spent the majority of his life in New Orleans. He served as an accountant for various hotels in downtown New Orleans and worked for the Bank of Louisiana as a Controller. Martin enjoyed golfing, cruising, fine dining and spending time with his family. He died unexpectedly from emphysema on June 13, 2015. He was survived by his wife, Ruby, his daughter, Tootie, and his son, Matthew.

Like Martin, Luis "Lucho" Sevilla also died in 2015. Lucho was a civil engineer in Nicaragua before he came to Louisiana to work as a structural engineer. Besides being technologically savvy, he had an artistic soul, enjoying oil painting. He painted portraits and pictures of prestigious places. In 2011, he discovered he had lymphatic cancer in one of his lungs. So he sought chemotherapy immediately. The treatment was successful. But the cancer came back; this time it attacked his other lung. In October 2014, he returned to chemo. However, the cancer advanced quickly, deteriorating his vital organs. Lucho died on November 20, 2015. He was survived by his wife, Mildred.

Ruby and Martin with Mildred celebrating Lucho's 62nd birthday. Gretna. July 8, 2011.

Lucho's first painting of a woman walking through the park in the rain. 1972.

Lucho's painting of the St. Louis Cathedral in the French Quarter. 1989.

This was Lucho's last painting. It's of a famous Louis Vuitton Journeys advertisement of Sofia and Francis Ford Coppola sharing a quiet moment in an Argentinian countryside. He painted it while he was receiving treatment at the University of Texas MD Anderson Cancer Center. It won a prestigious award. 2014.

Chapter 43: Josefana "Fanny" Norma

JOSEFANA "FANNY" NORMA was my elder sister by 2½-years. She lived in Nicaragua all her life except for the 2 years that she lived in New York with Martha and me from 1970–1971. Fanny died of complications from diabetes on February 5, 2016. She was survived by her son, William Perez Mendieta, and her daughter, Ana Julia Rodriguez Mendieta.

I have fond childhood memories of Fanny and me sharing a room, walking to school and doing our homework together, as well as playing games. She was a melancholic soul who liked to be quiet and left alone to draw and read poetry and introspect.

Fanny and me at Laguna de Xiloá. January 1970.

Chapter 44: Linkin Joie Delagneau

OUR SECOND GRANDSON—LINKIN JOIE DELAGNEAU—was born into this world on May 19, 2017 at 6:10 p.m. and died an hour later. He weighed 9.9 oz and was 9¼ inches long. The day prior, my daughter-in-law, Priscilla, went into the hospital for a scheduled anatomy scan of the baby. At first, the appointment went as expected: Linkin was healthy, moving around inside his mother's tummy. But nothing could have prepared us for the nightmare that was about to ensue. Priscilla's cervix had thinned-out while she was 2 cm dilated. That meant that she was in labor and would deliver soon. Priscilla called us immediately. Chester and I rushed to the hospital as we prayed for answers. Shortly after, I was allowed back to be with Jean Pierre and Priscilla.

God's mercy shrouded their decisions and everything that happened that day. Even the medical staff sensed God's presence through Priscilla's peace over the tragic situation. Tears were spilled and hugs were exchanged. God was in control.

Given the circumstances, Priscilla gave birth to Linkin. The nurse placed his tiny, warm body on her chest. Priscilla got to hold him and we got to talk to him.

Then, the doctor prepared us for the inevitable: because of his prematurity, his lungs were underdeveloped, and thus, he would not be able to breathe on his own, which meant he would pass away in just minutes. But, once again, God was merciful and kept Linkin breathing longer than expected.

About an hour later, Linkin slipped into eternity to see his heavenly Father face-to-face.

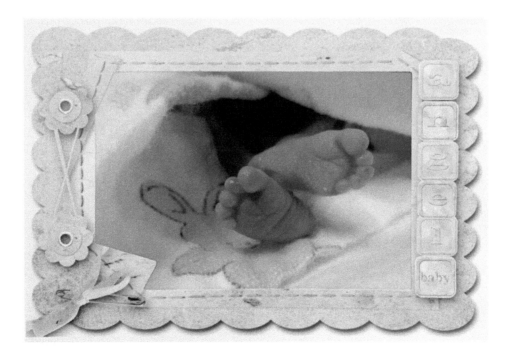

Linkin's angelic feet. May 19, 2017.

Picture of Linkin as a 2-year-old child in Heaven being held by an angel with the Holy Spirit hovering above them and with Jesus illuminating them with His love and light.

Drawn by Chestercito June 16, 2019 when Linkin would've already turned 2-years-old.

Chapter 45: Same Diagnosis, Different Conclusion

MY OLDER BROTHER—JOSÉ—was diagnosed with prostate cancer just like I. Unfortunately, he passed away from its death grip on June 12, 2017. He was surrounded by his loving family in New Orleans. His obituary reads: "He was a high school graduate from Instituto Pedagogico de Managua (La Salle) and graduated with a Bachelor's of Science in civil engineering (5 year curriculum) and later a Masters in Structures from Tulane University. In Nicaragua, as owner of IDECA [an engineering company], he was dedicated to the design and construction of several civil projects. In New Orleans he worked for Michael Grandolfi Engineering. He was introduced to the oil and gas industry in which he found his calling and where he dedicated most of his professional career. He was a member of the American Society of Civil Engineers (ASCE), the American Concrete Institute (ACI), and the American Institute of Steel Construction (AISC). He received many accolades, among them "The Manned Flight Awareness Honoree" presented by NASA at Kennedy Space Center. Jose is survived by his loving wife of 35 years, Maria Jose Parodi Delagneau, his children, Christine-Marie, Gerald, Jose Joaquin, Alexander, Damaris and Jose Rene."[51]

What I remember most about José is that he was a protective and caring older brother. He was always there for me whenever a problem arose. I also appreciated his articulate and well-poised manner of speaking. In short, José was a skilled orator. He loved to give speeches and recite poems at family parties. His passion for life also extended to oil painting, which he excelled at. Truth be told, everything José did was art.

Leslie's wedding. 2001.

---

[51] See https://www.legacy.com/obituaries/name/jose-delagneau-obituary?pid=185805078.

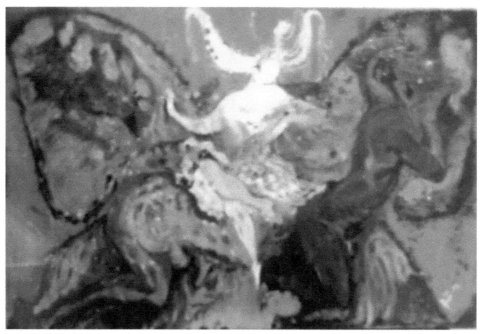

Oil painting by José called La Luciérnaga, which means "The Firefly." 1972.

Oil painting by José of a French Quarter courtyard in New Orleans. 1979.

Chapter 46: Sold!

AFTER YEARS OF COASTAL LIVING AND WATCHING SUNSETS OVER THE OCEAN, it was time for us to downsize and move inland once again in August 2017. Truth be told, we were sad to move. We had wonderful times in this house celebrating birthday parties, graduations, holidays, Sari and Chestercito's engagement, Sari's baby shower, Priscilla's baby shower, not to mention weekly barbeques and impromptu get-togethers. But we trusted in the Lord's provision for a new home.

That led us to Aliso Viejo to rent a small place as we continued our search for the perfect home. Two years later, with Jean Pierre as our realtor, we found the ideal home at 23622 Algiers St., Mission Viejo, 92691.

Inka Mama's Peruvian Cuisine Restaurant for Mother's Day. San Clemente. 2017.

Liuzza's with family. Left to right: Rainiero, Chester, me, Lida, Quincha, JP, Priscilla and Camilita.
New Orleans. October 19, 2017.

First Christmas at our Aliso Viejo home. 2017.

Chapter 47: Chi Mangia Bene, Vive Bene

CHI MANGIA BENE, VIVE BENE is an Italian saying that means "Who eats well, lives well." And the Delagneaus love to eat well. One of our favorite things to do with the people we love is to share a meal together. This allows us to relax and release the tensions from our stressful lives, relishing the delight we see on our loved ones' faces as they bite into something savory or sweet. Breaking bread together fills me—Myriam—with pleasure. It's how we're designed. The icing on the cake for me is that God also enjoys us enjoying life to the fullest. When we eat well and live well, He delights in us.

Family vacation. Eating lobster in Puerto Nuevo, Mexico. Vista Marina. July 25, 2018.

Thanksgiving with family in our Aliso Viejo home. November 22, 2018.

Celebrating Chester's 76th birthday at Stadium Brew Co. with family and friends. Left to right around the table: Camilita, JP, Priscilla, Sari, Damarita, José Tomás, Ed, Chestercito, Chester, Myriam, Nathanael and Carla. Aliso Viejo. December 21, 2018.

Celebrating JP's 42nd birthday at Outback Steakhouse with family. Laguna Hills. June 7, 2019.

Chapter 48: Book Launch Party!

RESEARCH, WRITE, REVISE. On repeat for years. But now the day had finally come when Chestercito would birth his baby, his theological text that he'd poured blood, sweat and tears into creating. And so, on Saturday, July 6, 2019, his devoted wife, Sari, threw him a book launch party to remember! With her sister's beautiful San Clemente home as the setting, friends and family poured in to celebrate Chester's monumental achievement. The house was festooned with decorative elements made from book pages and tables laden with food and drinks to ensure guests' enjoyment.

Pride and admiration filled my heart as I watched my son read an excerpt from his book and then sit behind a desk as family and friends lined up to have their book copies signed by the author. His five-year labor of love produced a remarkable work, titled *Biblical Ethics: An Exegetical Approach to a Morality of Happiness, Volume I: Old Testament Flourishing*. The heart of the book, as the title denotes, centers on the biblical concept of objective happiness, which entails virtuous living opposed to the postmodern view of happiness, which is subjective and thus relative. My favorite line of the book is found in the opening line of the Preface: "When we live the way we are supposed to, God is glorified and we are blessed (happy)!"

July 6, 2019.

Speaking.   Signing.   Smiling.

Chapter 49: Angelito Gabriel

OUR GRANDSON—GABRIEL NAVEED BANIMAHD—was born at 8:10 p.m. on November 1, 2018 at Hoag Hospital. He was a healthy baby weighing 6 lb, 9 oz. As the nurse placed him onto Crystal's chest, he grasped her finger, much to our delight as we witnessed the first bonding moments between mother and son. Blessed is the grandparent whose quiver is full of arrows (grandchildren).

These days, Gabriel ("Big G") keeps us active, running after him to keep him safe from his curious nature. But I'll never forget the scare we received during the second night of his stay in the hospital. He swallowed so much amniotic fluid that he began to choke, turning blue. Crystal screamed for the nurse who flew into the room with superhuman speed. She immediately flipped him upside down and patted his back expelling fluid in his lungs. After that day, Crystal was terrified of losing her son. For two days straight she stayed up all night watching him sleep.

Gabriel brings us much joy watching him dance and *caminar como un viejito*, which translates to mean "walk like an old man," just like his older cousin, Nathan, used to do.

Before leaving the hospital. November 3, 2018.

Auntie Mariann and Abuelita. San Clemente. February 5, 2019.

Aliso Viejo. May 29, 2019.

Mama holding "Big G." Mission Viejo.
October 12, 2019.

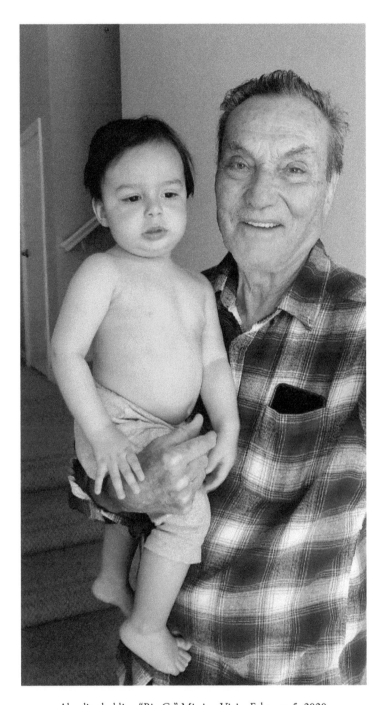

Abuelito holding "Big G." Mission Viejo. February 5, 2020.

Abuelita's 69th birthday. Mission Viejo.
March 13, 2020.

Abuelita holding "Big G." Mission Viejo.
March 24, 2020.

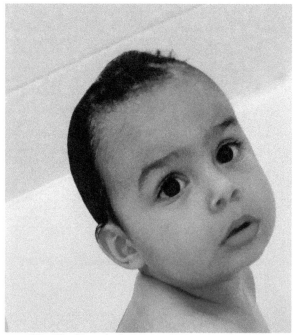

"Big G" taking a bath. Mission Viejo. May 28, 2020.

Chapter 50: Miracle Baby

OUR SECOND GRANDDAUGHTER—MIKAYLA SKYE DELAGNEAU—was born on July 31, 2019. JP and Priscilla had been praying daily for a baby after Linkin went to be with the Lord. So when Priscilla first found out she was pregnant, we all knew Mikayla was a miracle from God. But what we didn't know was the faith-testing journey they were about to encounter. Some days it was a daily dependence on God and other days it was a minute-by-minute dependency, not knowing if they were going to take their precious baby home from the hospital.

At just 18 weeks, at a routine checkup, Priscilla's cervix was once again thinning. She was put on immediate bed-rest and at 22 weeks her water broke while just lying in bed. They rushed to the hospital and the doctor said Priscilla would most likely deliver within 24 hours. The medical staff explained there was nothing they could do to save Baby Mikayla if she'd be born. We were all scared and confused, but Priscilla knew God had the power to save and make a miracle happen. She stayed on hospital bed-rest with no measurable fluid. The baby was still kicking and had a strong heartbeat. They made it to 24 weeks.

At midnight, Priscilla's contractions slowly started and Baby Mikayla was born at 3:45 a.m. She weighed only 1.6 oz and was quickly rushed to the NICU. We all knew God was working but, once again, we had no idea that the next journey was going to be even more difficult than the first. But in all of those moments, they saw God. Priscilla once said, "I felt God and I heard God."

Here is a list of some of the things they faced in their 111 day NICU stay:

- Level 1 brain bleeds
- Blood infection and 1 round of antibiotics
- Lung infection and 1 round of antibiotics
- Intestine infection and 2 rounds of antibiotics
- Heart murmur (that is now closed)
- Immaturity of the eyes (no surgery needed so far)
- Surgery for double hernia
- 109 days on oxygen (after several failed attempts she was finally off two days prior to coming home)

Mikayla is completely healthy. We will soon be celebrating her 1st birthday on July 31st. God is so good! She is our Miracle Baby and God is still writing her testimony. We are excited to see all He has planned for her life.

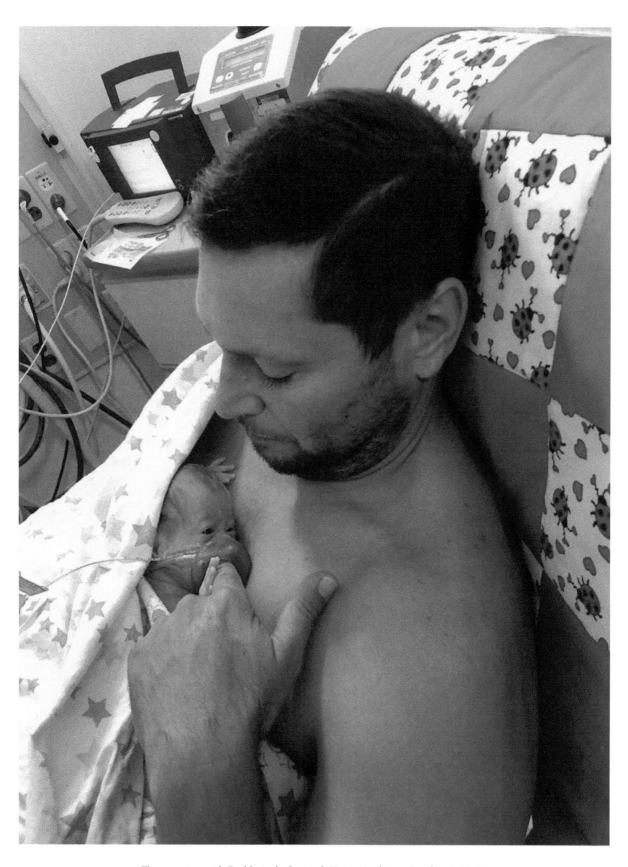

Tummy-time with Daddy in the hospital. Kaiser Anaheim. October 5, 2019.

NICU GRAD. November 19, 2019.

Pacifier Time. December 15, 2019.

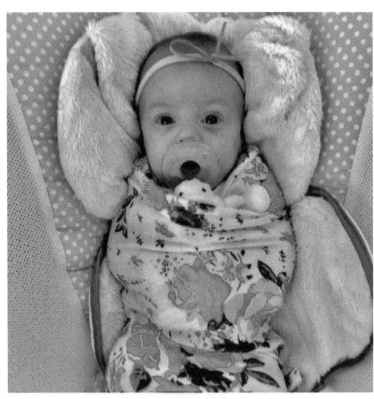

Swing Time. February 9, 2020.

Big Blue Eyes. May 13, 2020.

Camilita holding her l'il sister. July 1, 2020.

Mikayla's first birthday party. Laguna Niguel. July 31, 2020.

Chapter 51: "32 Years of Loyal Dedicated Service"

THE MOST PRESTIGIOUS AWARD one can receive for serving the elderly community in Southern California is the California State Assembly Award. With the assistance of a fantastic staff, Chester and I have been caring for the needs of the elderly in Mission Viejo for 32 years. Our dear friend, RCFE owner, administrator and 6Beds President, Ron Simpson, invited us to the 5th Annual Residential Care Facility for the Elderly (RCFE) Gala Banquet at the Sheraton Cerritos Hotel on Saturday, August 31, 2019. We gratefully attended.

We had so much fun that evening dining, dancing and celebrating our efforts as RCFE owners and administrators for over three decades. Crystalina, Sari and Chestercito joined us. The highlight of the night came when California assemblyman, Steven S. Choi, presented us with a plaque and certificate of recognition that reads, "In grateful appreciation of your 32 years of loyal and dedicated service to the frail elderly and individuals with special needs."

Enjoying a delicious dinner with family at the 2019 Gala Awards Banquet. Cerritos. August 31, 2019.

With Ron Simpson at the 2019 Gala Awards Banquet.

CERTIFICATE OF RECOGNITION

PRESENTED TO

CHESTER AND MYRIAM DELAGNEAU

IN HONOR OF BEING NAMED A

RESIDENTIAL CARE FACILITY FOR THE ELDERLY - OWNER AWRADEE WITH GLORIOUS HOMES, INC AT THE 6BEDS 5th ANNUAL GALA

In grateful appreciation of your 32 Years of loyal and dedicated service to the frail elderly and individuals with special needs. On behalf of the 68th Assembly District, I congratulate you on this accomplishment.

Proudly presented this 31st day of August, 2019

Steven S. Choi, Ph.D.
Assemblyman
68th District

Nice to be recognized.

Chapter 52: 4ᵗʰ of July

STARTING A BRAND NEW DECADE held for us hope and promise for the next chapter in our lives together. Little did we know at the dawn of the New Year that what lay ahead would soon be known as one of the strangest times in modern world history.

When the weight of the global pandemic known as Covid-19 hit with full force in mid-March of 2020, we found ourselves immersed in the most stringent caretaking protocols and restrictions that we had ever known in our 30+ years in the board-and-care business. We worked tirelessly to take every precaution so our residents would remain safe and healthy. Knowing what a blessing we were to the residents' families for the care we provide their loved ones, brought us pride and satisfaction. Nevertheless, one day in the not too distant future, we look forward to relinquishing our business' tremendous responsibilities and spending the next chapter of our lives snuggling our grandchildren and enjoying our beautiful family.

This past 4ᵗʰ of July, in particular, served as a reminder for how much we have to be grateful. After the social distancing precautions taken just a few months prior, it warmed our hearts to have our family and friends gather to barbecue, swim and socialize. Since city fireworks were cancelled, JP had purchased a fireworks collection so we could enjoy our own personalized show once the sun set. We loved watching Nathan's and Cami's faces light up with delight as the fireworks sparkled and hissed their multicolored display.

Certainly, the 4ᵗʰ of July is meaningful to all Americans, but perhaps even more so to those who know first-hand what it's like to have one's freedom and liberty stripped suddenly away. How often have we gazed up at the sky as a plane flew overhead and been reminded of what we left behind: the sights, the smells, the sounds, the feel of what we once knew so well. Yet in that same remembrance, comes the knowledge of what a plane once held for us, once meant for us, once did for us: it was a flight, a flight to freedom.

Enjoying the 4th of July with friends and family. From left to right: JP, Priscilla, Camilita, Brad, Ginny, Neal, Charis, Chester, Myriam, Sari, Nathan and Crystalina. (Chestercito took the picture.) Mission Viejo. 2020.

Acknowledgments

CHESTER AND I WOULD LIKE TO THANK OUR SON CHESTERCITO for giving our story a voice. He has spent hundreds of hours writing and editing—with the help of his brilliant and beautiful wife, Sari—not to mention collecting pictures and formatting the interior and exterior of this book for publication. Our mémoire is, no doubt, our legacy to our children, grandchildren, great-grandchildren, ad infinitum. Chestercito's literary assistance has made *Flight to Freedom* a heritage—far greater than money or gold—for others to read and remember and retell.

We'd also like to thank the following people who've contributed to this book by sharing stories and/or sending pictures to the editor: Crystal, Jean Pierre, Priscilla, Damarita, José Tomás, José René, Luis and Joseph Sterling, Mildred, Maria-José, Leslie Guill, Jared, Bob Blais, Ed Castro and Silvia Soto.

Lastly, we recognize that our success as board-and-care owners wouldn't be what it is today if it weren't for JP and Priscilla working for us as administrators for Glorious Homes #2. Their hard work and dedication to the elderly is much appreciated. And this family business is only special because we have special caregivers who take care of our residents—day and night, seven days a week—as if they were their own family. The Delagneaus are truly blessed!

Appendix A: Editor's Cut Pictures

Chester's family portrait. His mom is about 30-years-old and dad about 40-years-old. Managua. 1950s.

I sent this picture to my mother while I was at the club at the air force base in Managua. 1961.

Sixth grade at Colegio Bautista. Managua. 1966.

Myriam (18) modeling for world-renowned photographer Hernán Barquero, Jr. Managua. 1969.

Modeling Catalina bathing suit. Managua. 1969.

Myriam (19) modeling for world-renowned photographer Hernán Barquero, Jr. Managua. 1970.

Myriam (20) at a photo shoot on Mott Street. New York. 1971.

Chester holding Jr. (2-months-old) on the porch of our La Quinta home.
Christmas Day. Managua. 1973.

Nicaraguan Air Force Identification picture.
November 15, 1974.

Las Mercedes International Airport. Saying goodbye to family before they return to Louisiana.
Left to right: (back) Mildred, Lixio, Chimba, Rosa Lila, Myriam; (front) Jared, Leslie and Tootie. Managua.
1974.

At Uncle Federico's farm. La Quinta Los Angeles. 1976.

With our New Orleans family at Selva Negra Resort. Left to right: Rosa Lila, Mildred, Ruby, Lixio hugging Leslie, (front of Leslie) Chestercito, Chester, Lucho and Bob Blais. Matagalpa. 1977.

At Niudyl's country home on the eve of Damarita and José René's trip to New Orleans. Left to right: (back) José, me, Nilda, Mildred, José René, Dr. Humberto Porta, friend and Dr. Mario Porta; (front) Damaris, Myriam holding Chestercito, Niudyl and Lixio. Nindiri. May 13, 1978.

Ruby's house. Left to right: Mildred, Lucho, Lixio, Ruby, Chimba and Rosa Lila on his lap. Early 80s.

Ruby and Lixio visiting California. 1980s.

Costume party at the Arguello's home. Circa 1990.

Brothers. Left to right: my half-brother (David), José and me. New Orleans. August 26, 1991.

The Flamingo Hotel and Casino. Las Vegas. 2006.

Chestercito's 40th birthday party. Sari threw him a 1940s themed party.
October 2013.

Mother's Day with my three Loves at Saddleback Church San Clemente. May 8, 2015.

April 2, 2016.

Saddleback Church San Clemente with the family. October 28, 2018.

Front steps of the Hotel del Coronado. Left to right: (back) Chester, Sari, Thelmy, Oscar, Ricardo, Thelmita; (front) Nathanael, Camila, Sylvia and Myriam. August 3, 2019.

My sons wearing my pilot rings I gave them. Chestercito is wearing the Nicaraguan Air Force ring that reads, "Escuela Militar de Aviacion Guardia Nacional." JP is wearing the American Air Force ring that reads, "United States Air Force Pilot." Mission Viejo. July 24, 2020.

Best Friends. Left to right: Mario and Silvia Soto, the Delagneaus, and Karla and Ed Castro. Mission Viejo. July 25, 2020.

Appendix B: Glorious Homes' Letters of Recommendation

October 3, 1988

I am very happy to write a letter of recommendation for Glorious Home.

My mother, Kathryn Gasink, moved to Glorious Home in September, 1987. From the very beginning Chester, Myriam and their children made her feel like this was her home and she was part of their family. She has been included in all their family activities and parties, and she has always been treated with dignity and respect.

Myriam and Chester have taken such good care of my mom. I have never worried about the way she is being treated or cared for. My mother is a private person who tends to keep to herself. They respect that, but also encourage her to join in with group activities, such as bingo. They also have outings to the mall and go out to lunch or dinner.

My mother always looks wonderful. Myriam keeps her hair washed and styled, and even her fingernails are always polished. She is always dressed clean and neat, and made to feel good about herself. This isn't just when they know I am coming, but also when I drop in unexpectedly.

Chester and Myriam have notified me as soon as they suspect my mother isn't feeling well, and they are very conscientious regarding her overall health. Actually, they care for my mother the way I would if I could stay home with her.

Chester and Myriam are very sensitive, caring people who provide a positive, loving atmosphere for the people in their care. Without reservation I recommend Glorious Home to you.

Sincerely,

Sherry Drake

Sherry Drake

1/22/90

Dear Myriam,

Seeing how happy and very much at home my mother feels at your "Board & Care Home", has put my mind at ease & I'm very grateful.

Glorious Home is a very warm & family type home with very caring peopl taking care of those who need caring.

I thought it would be nice to let you know how happy I am about my mother being there.

Sincerely
Nina

9/27/90

Dear Chester & Miriam,

Thank you so much for the lovely chrysanthemum plant for Josephine's funeral service. It was thoughtful of you, also your presence there, Chester, was appreciated.

You folks took such good care of her, and showed her so much love. I know the Lord will bless you for the good work you are doing there.

If more mail comes there, please call us and we will pick it. We are anxious to get everything all settled up.

Sincerely,
John & Sylvia

Dear Myriam and Chester,   4/13/91

I wanted to write you soon and tell
how much I appreciate your kindness
during this very difficult week. It
must have been very trying for you
and your other guests, and I hope it
wasn't totally impossible for you all.

I want to write a kind, more "formal"
letter for your book, which I will do a
little later when I can think through
what I want to say. But I wanted to jot
this note to you right away to let you ~~know~~
know we love you and thank you for all
you have done, especially this last week.

I believe my grandmother was a Christian,
and there is comfort in knowing I will see
her again; but please pray for the
rest of my family as those "who have no
hope" of heaven (I Thessalonians 4:13-14).
Perhaps this will bring them to the
Savior!

Thanks again for your kindness.

Love in Christ, Sharon Awof

SHARON DEVOL

June 4, 1991

Mr. and Mrs. Chester Delagneau
25562 Gloriosa
Mission Viejo, CA 92691

Dear Chester and Myriam,

I am writing to thank you for your kindness in caring for my grandmother, Mary Dixon, over the past few years. During the times I visited her while she was living at the Gloriosa Home, I always found your staff to be pleasant and helpful.

It was the "little things" that you did which I'm sure made her time there more pleasant: applying make-up, dressing her fashionably, adding jewelry, fixing her hair nicely. Individual touches like these are what I would call "above and beyond the call of duty," and you were so kind to do this.

For the most part, my grandmother seemed happy and content there, and that was very important to us as a family. Your kind and gentle spirit, along with your sympathetic understanding, were very helpful to all of us under such difficult circumstances.

Thank you for being such a special friend and help to our family, especially to both my grandmother and grandfather. You have a very special home there!

Sincerely Yours,

Sharon M. Devol

August 17, 1997

Myriam and Chester Delagneau
25562 Gloriosa
Mission Viejo, CA 92691

Dear Myriam and Chester,

I want to thank you for your time and visits with my mother (Ruth Moses), my daughter (Jennifer) and I on August 7 and 9. We loved visiting *Glorious Home* and meeting you both. Dr. ElSanadi is definitely correct when he recommended your home as one of the best Board and Care's. You seem to really have a loving, caring environment. As we discussed, unfortunately my Mom "falls through the cracks." She needs more care than she has at *The Wellington*, but as higher functioning, a "Board and Care" is really not quite appropriate for her. Until my trip to California and some discussion and research, I did not know this.

Our current plan is to move my mother to Virginia to a relatively small, assisted-living establishment. The home is less than two miles from where I live and this will allow all us (my husband, Jennifer, our son, and our dog!) to visit Ruth often. I sincerely hope we can have this all work out.

Again, we wanted to thank you for your time and the wonderful visits. We all wish you the continued best success with *Glorious Home*. You are performing a most needed service and for this alone you should be most gratified.

Sincerely,

Elaine M. Stout

May 5, 2005

Chester & Myriam Delagneau
c/o Glorious Homes
24726 Argus Drive
Mission Viejo, CA   92691

Dear Chester & Myriam,

This letter is to acknowledge your faithful service, professionalism and extraordinary kindness in attending to my Mother's health and daily needs during the last 2-1/2 years of her life.

Both Shirley and Rina played significant roles in providing Mom extensive care, compassion, and friendship as her health steadily declined. We have so much respect for the difficult job these young women do without complaint each day.

As for you, the owners, how very humbled and grateful we are that you are a Christian family, having worked with us financially when times have been tough, and never increasing the cost of Mom's care in spite of her significant health care needs.

In the end, I particularly want to thank you for your love of our dear Mother, your love for the elderly, your heartfelt prayers and sensitivity to our family's suffering and your continued kindness throughout.

In closing, may I say on behalf of entire our family, we recognize Shirley and Rina for the extraordinary patience and care in doing their jobs each day and their special care of our dear Mother Hazel. The way they do their jobs is a pure reflection of your management. Each of you immeasurably contributed to Mom Hazel's quality of life, and, as a family, we "THANK YOU". She truly loved you all!

With Deep Appreciation,

Diane Wright & Family
Karen Hartman & Family
Susan Shehane & Family

Cc: Shirley & Rina

Encl: Obituary & Memory Card

288

Appendix C: Crystal, Jean Pierre and Chester Jr.'s Letters of Gratitude

Mom and Dad,

When I talk about your life experiences and everything you and Dad have gone through, people are shocked and say it sounds like a movie. When I listen to your stories, I feel a mixture of emotions, one of them being proud. You have both sacrificed so much for me and my brothers in order to give us a better life. I've never been the best at putting things into words but I want to thank you for your dedication, sacrifice and unconditional love you've given us. I am proud to be your daughter.

Love,

Crystalina

Mom and Dad,

This letter can only be written about you—the most amazing parents a son could ask for! I want to thank you for showing me love, support and unconditional love. In Nicaragua and America, you've sacrificed everything to give my siblings and me everything we could ever need. Thank you for being my biggest fans and for always believing in me. You took me to every soccer game and wrestling match, and you even woke up at dawn to take me surfing whenever I wanted. You've molded me into someone I can be proud of, and for that, I enjoy honoring you. Lastly, I want to thank you for introducing me to my Creator. I promise to teach my children the ways of the Lord and model the path for them, just as you have modeled it for me. You are and will always be my role models and my best friends. I thank God everyday for the parents he chose for me.

Love,

Jean Pierre Delagneau

Mamita y Chaleoncito,

It took me a long time to truly appreciate everything you've sacrificed for my siblings and me. For many years I roamed this earth angry because of how my life turned out, and sadly I blamed it on you. It took a bona-fide miracle to soften the hardened soil of my ungrateful heart. Becoming a Christian was the paradigm shift I needed to see the world through your pilgrim eyes. Now, I understand that you were trying to survive with two small children when you came to America. I have no doubt that you both did the best you could to nurture us—given the circumstances the Lord had provided. Young and inexperienced, you displayed faith, strength, courage, honor, hope, determination, selflessness and unconditional love as you worked, at times, odd and multiple jobs, just to feed and clothe us. Now that I have a son of my own, I understand the depth and length of your self-sacrifice to provide for and protect us.

What I believe this angry world needs is to hear your story—a story of loyalty, ingenuity and never giving up on your children, your marriage and your faith. You've modeled for your family, friends and everyone you know the true meaning of faith ("the reality of what is hoped for, the proof of what is not seen" Hebrews 11:1, CSB), while maintaining a joyous disposition. Your story will forever be told because it mirrors the greatest story ever told—the story of our Lord and Savior, Jesus Christ, who was faithful to a young Diriamban girl and a Masayan boy many, many years ago.

Con Mucho Amor y Cariño,

Chestercito

Appendix D: "Suitcase of One" Poem

This poem is about surviving Nicaragua's Civil War. By Chester J. Delagneau, Jr.

Suitcase of One

Saying goodbye in 1979, we left our father and motherland behind.

"Will we ever see you alive again and feel your fraternal embrace?
And if not, how long before we forget the sound of your voice,
Your high cheekbones and your fearless face?"

Courage and strength led you by your fists to stay and fight
Contra communism and atheism,
All for freedom—
Freedom of family, faith and individualism.

Packing for three in a suitcase of one,
My mother, brother and I piled into a cramped space
Liked frightened cattle
Leaving the Latino race
Of our ancestors and anarchists—
Nicaraguan realists and idealists.

"Will we make it to America, Mama?
And if so, how will we survive its political drama,
Which in time will recreate
The hate we fought so hard to escape?"

Courage and strength motivated your maternality
To sustain us—not by begging
But by making *masa* for *nacatamales*
Wrapped in banana leaves
To sell on the streets of New Orleans.

Crying for normalcy and belonging in a country that doesn't recognize my sadness,
Only my immigrant status,
I fail to make eye contact with the Whites—
Tomorrow's tycoons of industry,
Tomorrow's Great Gatsby socialites.

"Will I survive in this strange land of liberty and opportunity,
While I stumble my words with broken Englishy,
Wishing I'd been a better brother,
Feeling always like the minority?"

Honor and strength now calls on me.
Together they tuck me in and lull me to sleep at night
With a soft coo that soothes my memories
Of the deceptive destruction a civil war had
On my proud Hispanic family,
A war that created a cultural dissonance within me,
A war that made me what I am today—
A warrior poet of freedom and truth,
A voice for the forgotten,
A voice for today's disgruntled youth.

Written November 8, 2019

Appendix E: "The Gardener" Poetic Prose

Chestercito wrote this in his blog (chesterdelagneau.com) about the only true solution to communism.

The Gardener

Capitalism will never defeat communism. Capitalism might prove to be a better politico-economic system of government, but it's powerless in and of itself to deracinate communism's destructive roots, which choke the life of all diversity, drive, competition and nutrition in a garden that's designed as a feast for the eyes and stomach.

Only with scarred hands that till the arid, hardened soil of communism's internment can we enjoy life in a gratuitous garden replete with colorful diversity and healthy competition that inspires us to reach for the heavenly hands that created us to hold.

Only a providential mixture of organic matter and minerals created *ex nihilo*—that feeds from the Light—can decompose communism's pseudo-acts of humanism.

Only the Gardener with thorn-pricked thumbs and dirt under his fingernails can uproot the weeds of totalitarianism in order to cultivate creative acts of true humanism in the soft, humble soil of sacrificial love.

Written October 29, 2019

Life can only be understood backwards; but it must be lived forwards.
—Søren Kierkegaard

9 781087 899466